C0-CCG-865

DECORATIVE SCULPTURE

DECORATIVE SCULPTURE

SELECTED BY
GEORG KOWALCZYK
WITH AN INTRODUCTION
BY
AUGUST KÖSTER
OF THE STATE MUSEUM BERLIN

MCMXXVII
E. WEYHE, 794 LEXINGTON AVE. NEW YORK

PRINTED IN GERMANY

CONTENTS

EGYPT AND THE NEAR EAST
Page XIII

GRAECO-ROMAN
Page XVIII

EARLY
CHRISTIAN AND BYZANTINE
Page XXVI

ROMANESQUE
Page XXVIII

GOTHIC
Page XXXI

THE RENAISSANCE
Page XXXIII

ISLAM
Page XXXVI

ANALYSIS OF PLATES

EGYPT
Plates 1–14

THE NEAR EAST
Plates 15–31

GRAECO-ROMAN
Plates 32–123

EARLY
CHRISTIAN AND BYZANTINE
Plates 124–159

ROMANESQUE
Plates 160–201

GOTHIC
Plates 202–235

THE RENAISSANCE
Plates 236–288

ISLAM
Plates 290–320

INTRODUCTION

Egypt and the Near East

Though Egyptian art is not the most ancient that is known to us it was the first to influence that of Europe to a predominating extent. It would be impossible to conceive occidental art without that of Egypt, the influence of which is still felt to-day. Egyptian, like every other art, had its tap-roots in religious cult, and the Egyptian sacred edifices were erected in honour of the gods and the dead. However, the main object of early art in Egypt was not at first to erect beautiful edifices, but such as would merely serve the purposes of cult. Representations of the human form and of gods, as seen in the temples and tombs, are supposed to embody the deities or the souls of the dead. They serve to record scenes and events as required by the Egyptian cult, and they were also supposed to please the deities as well as the souls of the departed. The action itself is the main point, not artistic quality. Hence it is immaterial whether the figures are simple contours, coloured wall-paintings, or carved stone reliefs. Nay, the latter were, at least in the earliest periods, nothing more than paintings rendered more enduring by being carved; for the plastic representations of scenes were coloured. These reliefs tended more and more to be purely decorative, and were more carefully and artistically designed. The marked desire to attain to artistic perfection is conspicuous, though the result falls short of the aspiration. This desire, however, proves the inherent artistic character of the Egyptians.

The oldest known Egyptian works of art date from about 5000 B. C., but they must have been preceded by a much longer period of development, the length of which cannot be estimated. The artist had long since mastered the technique of depicting what he wanted to describe. From draughtmanship he had passed to painting, and later on to relief carving, and his art is already employed decoratively in ornamenting small utensils and votive-offerings by means of carvings in slate, wood, and ivory. They represent the most ancient expression of decorative sculpture.

It was only a thousand years later that plastic art was employed to embellish architecture. But brick had first to be replaced by stone before architectural decoration was feasible, though it was only employed on a small scale. A leading characteristic of the Egyptian temple is that its unity is not destroyed by details, and that its decorative members never detract from its monumental character. The outer walls are massive and unembellished. The wealth of ornamant is concentrated in the interior where the circular column is the leading feature. Its ancestor was the square order. It is purely decorative and endeavours to conceal its constructional use, namely that it is actually a support carrying the beams. It takes the shape of plants: palms, papyrus, lotus, etc.; that is to say of plants, which, with the exception of the palm, could not serve for supports. The capital also strives to counterfeit the palm-top, lotus blossoms, papyrus umbel as well as its buds, though rather indicated than developed. Any attempt at detail would diminish the grandeur of the whole, especially as the measurements are often gigantic. The decorative effect of the colossal columns is almost fabulous. With their huge bulk they resemble mighty Titans from some unknown world.

In the earliest periods only the palm capital was sculptured and the details of the leaves hewn in the stone. Later on the capitals were more richly embellished and often shaped to imitate bunches of flowers interspersed with buds.

The interiors of the temples contained rows of statues of the Pharaohs. Sometimes the exteriors were ornamented with enormous figures, as for instance the rock-cut temple of Aboo Simbel, where the sitting Pharaoh colossi are most imposing.

The sculptor subordinated himself to the rigid laws of an architecture in which horizontal and vertical lines dominated. The stony calmness and solemn quietude prevailing in these halls were not to be disturbed by the statue, hence the austerity of the figures.

Sphinxes and similar animals with human heads embody symbolic ideas. Whole rows of these figures are placed in front of the temples and form an avenue leading up to them, or connect two sanctuaries one with another. The main road to the Temple of Ammon at Karnak is an avenue of recumbent rams each holding an image of the deity or of the Pharaoh between its front legs. In other places lions' bodies with human heads — usually male — are favoured. The female sphinx is of a later date.

The mural paintings which ornament the walls of the sacred edifices in the shape of low-relief sculpture in intaglio retained their religious and symbolic signification during the whole period of Egyptian culture to a much greater extent than did the sculptures in the round. As integral parts of the architecture the effect of these reliefs is of pronounced decorative character, and they may therefore be regarded from our point of view as decorative sculpture in the best sense of the word. But they are neither conceived as works of art nor as decorative ornamental members, for their purpose is solely to record events, of which there is, indeed, a sufficiency, and there is hardly a phase of daily life in Egypt with all its minutiae and details, which is not depicted on these surface decorations.

Sculpture is largely employed for decorative purposes in arts and crafts. Beginning with the primitive carvings of the ancient Empire, numerous utensils were plastically ornamented during successive centuries. The carved ivory legs of furniture are shaped in imitation of animals' legs; the chair-arms represent recumbent lions; mirror-handles burgeoning blossoms. The handles of vessels resemble the bodies of lithe animals, and the bodies of slim girls in a swimming posture serve as handles of small ointment boxes. Countless motifs of a similar character are employed for ornamental purposes on all sorts of utensils beginning with the carefully incised animal's head on the prow of the royal yacht down to the most delicately carved minute insect forming part of a necklace or hair-ornament. These ornaments are always supremely perfect in technique and are imbued with a profound artistic spirit.

* * *

The countries drained by the Tigris and Euphrates supplied but little material to the architect and sculptor which they could employ for edifices and statues. There was neither stone nor wood. But the country provided an unlimited supply of reeds and clay, and the architect was able to construct monumental buildings even out of this material by using it in enormous quantities.

The clay bricks, usually sun-dried, were not very substantial; hence it was necessary to erect walls, the thickness of which was a third of their height. In the case of fortresses — and all edifices of great magnitude were more or less fortresses — the walls were still thicker; many even twenty meters, in some cases more. Their tops were so wide that they could be used as roads, and they exceeded the width of the main thoroughfares in our modern cities.

The system of building was very advantageous for dwelling-houses as the intolerable heat could not easily penetrate such massive walls. And it was easy to provide cool apartments, providing the ceilings were equally thick.

The interior decoration of Babylonian houses was limited to carpets, curtains, or water-colours painted on the stucco facings of the clay walls. A threshold from Khorsabad shows that in later periods the carpet patterns served as models for decorative sculpture (P. 28).

The outer walls were not at first ornamented. But the projecting towers (usually square) placed at regular intervals were distinctly rhythmic features, though perhaps not intentionally so. They were often reproduced on a small scale to ornament lesser edifices, and were then diversified by numerous recesses.

The gates, which were of great strategic value, afforded considerable scope for decorative treatment. They were strengthened by towers and soon decorated in such a manner as to develop a peculiar form of ornamental portal sculpture.

Oriental art always favoured fabulous monsters as symbols of evil powers. They were employed both to decorate and protect the gates and portals of the fortresses, palaces, and temples. As statues in the round they are mainly stone lions or celestial animals with human heads; as coloured brick reliefs they represent wild bulls or griffin-like dragons.

The early reliefs are not meant to record events like those of Egypt, but to bear witness to the greatness of the monarch whom they depict as an all-powerful and sublime being guarded by gods and demons. The sculptor's aim is to express the sovereign's power and his physical superiority. But, owing to a complete neglect of the nude, he was not able, as was his Greek confrère, to convey the idea of superiority by representing a perfect body. His sole mode of expression was to portray the king as victor in his fights with demons, dragons, and similar beasts. But the way these creatures are depicted proves the skill of the artist. The coloured dragons and wild bulls flanking the portals seem so real, in spite, of their fantastic forms, that one is almost convinced they must have existed. Over five hundred of these figures (P. 18) — each eight feet long — decorated the Ishtar Gate. Rows of wild bulls and dragons alternated one with another. These crowds of statues with their riot of colour: white, red, yellow, and green on a blue background, must have been most effective.

The greatest scope is given to the artist in the magnificent Assyrian reliefed mural decoration in which the highest perfection of Near Eastern art was attained to, and which will always be considered as supreme masterpieces (P. 20 *et seq.*). As they replaced water-colour mural paintings on the stuccoed clay-brick walls we should remember that these reliefs were also coloured. They depict battles and victories, transport of troops, fording of streams, camp life, sieges, storming of hostile fortresses, etc. But hunting and all its accompanying events are also represented. The most successful portrayals are those of animals, especially of horses (Pp. 20—24). These reliefs prove such a love of animals, such a great power of observation of structure and movement, so profound a knowledge of horsemanship, and such an admirable knowledge of horse-training that only a rider is able to fully appreciate them. In these reliefs the human form is also more natural and more freely interpreted. This will be recognized in the riders' attitudes which could only have been reproduced as the result of the sculptor's great power of observation (Pp. 20—23).

This ability to observe also enabled the sculptor to offer a more powerful and lifelike representation of the rest of the animal world. Just as the Dutch marine painters of the 17th century took part in the battles they painted, so too did the Assyrian artists participate in the chase in order to study animals in their native haunts; for instance the wild sow (P. 25) moving through the thicket with her young, or the herd of wild asses hunted by powerful hounds (P. 24). Even the most transitionary movement has been caught, as for instance a galloping jenny turning to watch her foal unable to keep up with the herd. It would be difficult to find more magnificent representations of lions than those of the Assyrian artists. In the great animal parks which, according to Xenephon, were kept by the rulers, and in which lions were preserved and hunted, the artist had an opportunity to observe the king of the beasts. What modern artist has ever succeeded in portraying an animal so movingly as that famous lioness dragging herself along with a javelin in her spine (P. 21), or the trapped animal, which on leaving its cage in the park, thinks it has regained its liberty? Naturally all the work was not of an equally high quality as it was intended for decorative purposes and hence not always executed by first-rate artists.

A local variant of Near Eastern art was that of the Hittites which for a time developed independently and attained to a certain perfection under Egyptian influence. But at first the Hittite was not possessed of high technical skill, hence the crude appearance of his work, which, however, does not lack certain decorative qualities (Pp. 29—31).

Persian art was also at first influenced by that of Egypt and later by Graeco-Ionic art, thus the Persian columned hall was the outcome of contact with Egyptian architecture. However, the Persians' spirit of independence and creative ability are proved by their not copying the shape of the columns, but inventing their own highly decorative column base with Near Eastern motifs.

The Phoenicians were not imbued with a creative spirit in art. Their work consists mostly of a fusion of heterogeneous decorative details borrowed from various countries (Pp. 33, 34).

* * *

Graeco-Roman

The Greek attitude towards works of art is quite different from that of the Egyptian. With the latter the decisive factor in the creation and employment of ornamental forms is always a mystical symbolism. It is typical of the cheerful and sunny character of the Greek that he should limit himself to decoration and ornament pure and simple. The artistic aesthetic factor is one and all to him. But however generously the Greeks may employ ornamental forms, they never do so at the expense of truth and clarity; that is to say, the Greek classic period never made use of ornamental form, however picturesque, in order to employ it decoratively in an illogical, incomprehensible or false manner. The Greek, to take an example, does not carve a mat-work band when there is nothing to be held by it, or when there is no justification for such ornament. In later periods, especially in those of Roman art, all pretensions to a logical employment of ornament were renounced, but such was the refined taste of the epoch that it was possible to freely employ numerous decorative ornamentations without introducing a note of disharmony. Nay, works were created in this manner, the decorative effect of which was perfectly charming.

Greek architecture begins with the monumental edifice: the royal palace and the temple. Both were already richly ornamented in the most ancient period, and doubtlessly the effect of the riot of colours they displayed was most impressive. And when marble replaced wood and brick the magnificence of the temples grew in magnitude. The painter was succeeded by the sculptor. Sculpture was soon pressed into service to ornament architecture. But it was never deprived of the many colours it had inherited from its predecessor painting. We should always remember this fact if we wish to realize the full effect of antique ornamental forms. The manner in which the Greeks employed colour, especially on statuary, shows very clearly that the decorative motif alone was the decisive factor. They applied their colours quite independently of nature and reality. Blue horses or oxen did not strike them as being unnatural. But their constructional honesty, which aimed at emphasizing every function of the architectural members, went so far that, in spite of their love of decorative ornament, column and architrave were at first left without ornamentation.

It was only the Ionic capital (P. 41) with its extraordinary effective volutes and its subordinated decorative elements that softened to a certain degree the rigid architectural standards hitherto obtaining.

The Ionic order first introduces a shaft with a base. In its inception it is perfectly simple, consisting, at it does, of a circular convex member, a concave one, and a smaller convex member above. When edifices were elaborately enriched by plastic ornament the bases were also decorated. A closely plaited mat-work band is carved in the marble of the upper convex member and completely encircles it. The bases of ancient Greek columns differ considerably from still earlier and simpler examples. Octagonal or twelve-sided slabs are inserted below the bases and carved with a diversity of low-reliefs on each face.

There can be little doubt that the decorative effect of the Ionic capital is exceeded by that of the Corinthian (P. 41) in which the highly picturesque leaves of the acanthus surround a basket-like nucleus and, in spite of their formal grouping, are both airy and free. Behind the acanthus leafage the upward thrust of the tendrils support the flat abacus.

The anta corresponds to the column as a supporting factor in architecture. It was originally a vertical wooden beam terminating the side walls and protecting them. It soon developed into an artistic feature. The horizontal tripartition: a frieze of hanging palmettes framed above and below by powerful ovolo mouldings is characteristic of the ancient Ionic anta capital (P. 40). The narrow sides have three flat volutes superimposed one on the other.

The pilaster capitals, which were used to crown wall-shafts, are akin to the antae capitals. Antique artists decorated them with gracefully curved volutes (P. 43). Their upper projection suggests the capital motif. The centre, or "eye", of the volute is rosette-shaped and the space between the spiral scrolls is filled with two palmettes projecting out of the volutes. Page 42[1] shows how this volute motif developed, and what it looked like two centuries later.

The richest decorative ornament of the Greek temple is concentrated in the upper part. The artist could give free play to his imagination in ornamenting the frieze, pediment, and roof with plastic motifs. And we see how he managed to convey a picturesque idea of a scene taken from mythological or epic subjects by means of small groups consisting of only two or three figures (P. 37). The artist who adorned the metopes was often influenced by examples of monumental sculpture. The metopes sometimes came from the workshops of the greatest sculptors who, however, probably were not the designers. Among the ancients there was not the hard and fast line between art and handicrafts as obtains to-day. This is no doubt one of the main reasons for the wonderful development and high standard of decorative sculpture.

It was from Ionia that the custom of decorating the upper part of the cella wall with a frieze or horizontal band of sculpture was introduced. Later on this ornamental band was carried over the columns on the outside This offered an opportunity of presenting a continuous scenic action, a favourite method of ornamentation with the ancient craftsmen. It was from painting that Greek sculpture borrowed its manner of composition and grouping, and it was just in composition that the frieze reliefs attained to their greatest perfection, as for instance in those of the Pergamon altar.

The projecting roof of the temples was especially emphasized by the employment of decorative ornamentation. Thus the raking cornice of the pediment is decorated with guttae which are often carried round the sides of the building. In order to drain the rain-water off the roof the cyma was no longer pierced by holes, but projecting terracotta spouts were added. These simple conduits were finally replaced by an ornamental figure, usually a lion's head (P. 48) with the mouth wide open. Sometimes rams' and dogs' heads, as well as masks were employed (*cf.* Pp. 51, 64, 66, 67).

The corners and summits of the gables were ornamented with antefixae or acroteria. The antefixae were first used to hide the ends of the ridges on the roof. They were originally richly ornamented discs, and then developed into plastically formed palmettes. The more elaborate buildings favoured marble acroteria. The ornamental form was richer, the palmettes were more exuberant, or even replaced by figures such as panthers and sphinxes (Pp. 33, 50) or the statue of the pinioned goddess Nike. The pediment acroterium of the Aegina temple (P. 46) is particularly rich in its combination of ornament and figures. It consists of a bold foliage ornamentation with numerous palmettes, beside which are the figures of two girls in the style of the 6th century. The connection between the figures and the ornament seems to be somewhat loose and inorganic. We can see how beautifully the motif of combined foliage ornament and figures developed by a glance at the corner antefix of the Pergamon altar (P. 46): Nike rises from a magnificent acanthus chalice surrounded by exuberant foliage which seems to cling protectingly around her.

The antique craftsman not only had marble at his disposal for decorative purposes, but also above all bronze. Judging by the number of bronze works that have been preserved, they seem to have been made in great profusion. The art of working in metal is of extreme antiquity, and the Greek artist was already an expert in the technique of metal embossing at a very early period. Casting metal was introduced later. Bronze was not only used for making arms, but also for vessels such as: pots, bowls, pails, cans, jugs etc. which were adorned with plastic ornament, above all the handles. The early types were often oriental in style. The lion was employed in all variations and sizes. When used on a vessel or implement (P. 34[1]) he was represented in stiff and antique heraldic attitudes. Pan-handles were made in imitation of a lion saltant. Some handles were shaped like a lioness striking her prey with her paw (P. 70). The lion is the origin of the chimera (P. 55, 68). He vested sphinxes (Pp. 33, 50) and griffins (Pp. 44, 78[2], 72, 79[1]) with his body, and numerous other fabulous animals claim him as their ancestor. Another motif borrowed from oriental art, and of pronounced decorative effect, was the griffin, a fabulous animal with a lion's body and an eagle's head. It is met with in Egypt, among all oriental peoples, and came to Greece from Syria via Asia-Minor as early as the 8th century. Earlier art favoured heads in plastic ornament, some embossed (P. 36[2]) some cast. A typical ornament was a large eagle's head with wide-open beak, long ears and a button-like conventionalized protuberance on its forehead. The eyes were made of glass paste or enamel. Griffins' heads were only employed for decorative purposes on bronze kettles, and were fixed on the upper edge with the heads turned outwards. When the whole figure of a griffin was represented, it was either in a sitting or striding posture, as a rule with the front paw raised, the enormous wings folded. When two griffins were employed for ornamental purposes they were placed opposite each other in a heraldic posture. An ornament (P.44) or vase (P.79[2]) was inserted between them. A particularly beautiful bronze handle is shaped like a griffin fighting a serpent (P. 71).

The head of a ram (P.49), being a specially attractive motif owing to the shape of the skull and curved horns, was often used in bronze plastic ornament. And four such heads fastened to the edge of a large bronze bowl serve as handles. Owing to the fact that it was not possible to cast more than one form from the same wax model — in contradistinction to modern bronze casting — it was necessary to make a new model each time, and for this reason two such head pendants were never quite alike. Each piece was, as it were, an original, and therefore *per se* a distinct work of art, hence the artistic effect of the whole. But antique bronzes were not originally coated with a more or less glossy dark green patina, as we imagine them to have been, and as they are to-day; rather were they of a bright golden hue.

The decorative art of the Hellenistic-Roman epoch, that is to say of the post-Alexandrian period, affords a picture that differs consideraby from that of the classic epoch. Owing to changed conditions quite different premises obtained for the development of art. A close connection had been established with the Orient, and had familiarized the Occident with its peculiarities and conditions. International trade maintained the connection. The numerous cities founded by Alexander, partly inhabited by Greeks and Orientals, facilitated a growing amalgamation of the two cultures. Magnificent capitals with splendid monumental edifices rose in the various autonomous countries of the disintegrated empire. And to the same extent that the standard of life became freer, more liberal and wealthy, so too did art with all its details down to even the most minute ornament. Figures and ornaments such as heads, masks, and heads of the Medusa are more frequently met with, also figures in transitionary attitudes and movements such as the griffin fighting the serpent (P. 71[2]) or the dwarf struggling with the crane.

Amongst others, realistic bronze figures are characteristic Alexandrian miniature works of art. Reliefs are used as mounts or to ornament grave monuments and funeral urns, etc. Preference is given to scenes of daily life such as the artist observed in the streets of the city with its variety of different nationalities: street-singers, lute-players, jugglers, dancers, and all sorts of hawkers and pedlars. Page 62 shows us the fisherman as he could often be seen on the Nile. He is sitting naked on the bank and is about to land a fish. The second relief depicts him running through the streets with two baskets slung from a long pole and offering his fish for sale.

It was during the reign of Augustus that Rome enjoyed a period of tranquillity that was highly favourable to the development of art. It is true that the attitude of the Roman towards art differed from that of the Greek. For the former it was above all a means of displaying decorative splendour, and for this reason he chiefly concentrated his attention on architecture. Though the Romans were at first influenced by Etruscan art, they gradually turned to the Greek examples. At the time of the Roman Empire Greek models were the standard, although one does not always encounter the Greek sense of form.

The Ionic capital in Rome was at first nearly quite Greek in character in accordance with the example set by Asia-Minor, but the ornamentation soon becomes richer. An ornate band of decoration is carved on the neck, and the coussinets are ornamented with the leaves of reeds or acanthus (P. 108[2]). The so-called diagonal capital, already evolved in Hellenic times and in which the coussinet was omitted and the volutes made to do duty for four faces (P. 108[1]), is employed by the Romans, but greatly enriched.

The Corinthian style, which tended more towards the ornate, appealed to Roman taste, and for this reason was much favoured by Roman architects. Here too the Greek example serves as a model, but much of its grace and beauty were lost (P. 41[2], 109[1]). The space between the ascending scroll ornament offered the sculptor an opportunity to enrich the capital. The flower over the small wreaths (P. 41[2]) is carried up to the abacus. The small tendrils are thrust upwards, and palmette-like leaves (P. 109[1]) or flowers joined by tendrils (P. 107[1]) are inserted under them (P. 109[1]). The capital has a most beautiful decorative effect in its more elaborate development, when even the abacus is embellished with plastic ornament (P. 109[2]). The composite order, which originated in Rome, presents a new motif. It consists of the Corinthian leafage, above which an Ionic capital with large angle volutes is inserted. The abacus with its central rosettes betrays the fact that it is borrowed from the Corinthian order. The more elaborate composite capitals have volutes with plastic leafage.

It was seldom possible for the Romans to imitate the Greek temple frieze on their own edifices because their artists were not capable of composing a series of figures of the length required for a temple frieze. The talent of the Roman sculptor lay in another direction: the decorative-ornamental. For this reason, with but few exceptions, he treated the frieze from a purely ornamental point of view. The Augustan period favoured a continuous band of foliage ornament; and numerous decorative motifs owe their origin to this epoch. Between the foliage festoons, above which beautiful flowers were placed, the artist inserted winged cupids, Nikes and birds (P. 105[4]). Masks, heads and animals rise from the flower chalices. The leafage festoons are often spaced by means of animal figures, fabulous monsters, etc. in heraldic postures. Vases, candelabra and baskets of fruit were inserted between them (P. 97). Cupids or bucrania supporting festoons decorate the frieze as they often do sarcophagi. Another motif consists of decoratively grouped arms, paterae etc., also interrupted by bucrania (P. 112). The Romans enriched the cornice by the addition of a new member: the console. It is in reality a conventionalized beam-end treated decoratively (P. 112). The lower part of the console was ornamented with a broad mat-work band framed in bead moulding or an acanthus leaf. The side facets were decorated with two volutes, the centres of which contained rosettes and flowers.

Of all decorative motifs in Roman plastic art the acanthus is doubtlessly the most frequently employed. The leaves are grouped in such a manner as to represent large chalices (P. 96) out of which plant and figure ornaments project, or they are arranged as beautiful scroll ornaments with full-blown flowers (P. 73, 97), closed and burgeoning buds. Very often cupids, Nikes, and similar figures (P. 83, 100), birds (P. 105), insects and other creatures, fruit and baskets of fruit (P. 97) are interspersed among the chalices and scroll ornament.

Decorative sculptural art not only favoured acanthus, but also numerous other plant motifs such as conventionalized leaves, flowers, stalks and fruit (P. 81, 104), or a naturalistic (P. 86[2], 101) interlacement of leafage and flowers often variegated with other motifs. In the time of Augustus artists favoured the laurel (P. 75[1]), as well as oak-leaves with acorns (P. 80). The honeysuckle is conventionalized to represent a palmette. Vine with grapes, bindweed, lilies, poppies, hawthorn, pumpkin-blossoms and ears of wheat (P. 81, 105[1]) serve to decorate cinerary urns (P. 74[2], 75[2]). The ornamentation of the pilasters and candelabra is particularly charming and consists mainly of beautiful clustering naturalistic leafage ornament (P. 101). This type of decoration belongs to the most beautiful creations of antique ornamentation.

When employed to ornament grave altars and sarcophagi, as well as candelabra and tripod bases, the various motifs are combined to form festoons of fruit and flowers supported by figures. The motif was doubtlessly borrowed from the altar decorated with festoons of real flowers, or from the decorated balustrades of the temples upon which such festoons were first carved in marble. Hermogenes (2nd half of the 3rd century B. C.) had already ornamented the balustrade of the Temple of Artemis in Magnesia with festoons supported by stags' heads. This pattern soon became very popular. The stag's head was presently replaced by the more effective ox-skull (bucranium) (P. 81). Now and again the ancient motif of the ram's head was revived to support the festoon (P. 78[2]). Sometimes preference is given to other heads or masks for this purpose. Even complete figures, such as pinioned Nikes or cupids (P. 79[2]), are features of a more exuberant ornamentation. Hermogenes had already filled the space over the encarpus with conventionalized paterae (P. 81), the shape of which was not unlike a rosette or stylicised flower. Sometimes this space is filled with wind-blown ribbons (P. 95), masks (P. 79[2]), heads of the Medusa, and later with portrait busts in scallop shells, eagles or other animals. The *corona civica* (the Roman civic crown made of the leaves that grew on the oak sacred to Jupiter) was a favourite motif. It was a much valued prize in the early days of the Empire, and was frequently reproduced on altars, *e.g.* on the altar (P. 80) dedicated to Jupiter by Scipio Orfitus (*circa* 295 A. D.).

With the growth of luxury in public life, private residences became more and more ornate and magnificent. The reception halls — the atrium and dining-room — were gorgeously fitted with furniture which was more for show than use. Some pieces were made of bronze, some of marble, or other rare stone, and exuberantly ornamented. Vases-de-luxe of all sizes and shapes (P. 73), candelabra, marble tables (P. 103), thrones (P. 102), large water bowls, tripods, etc. filled the apartments. Lions, sphinxes, griffins, and other fabulous monsters, as well as human figures in the shape of caryatides, supported the furniture, and the finer examples were extremely decorative.

The idea of replacing the pilaster and column by a human figure as decorative motif is of Greek origin. It has been handed down to succeeding centuries, and the architecture of all ages made use of the caryatide. Antiquity favoured draped female figures standing in restful postures with their arms hanging loosely at their sides. On their heads they bore a cushion-like capital supporting the entablature. Another equally attractive type was a maiden sustaining the entablature with one hand (P. 99).

The terracottas, called "Campana reliefs", after the Campana collection, which contained numerous examples of these works of art, were a peculiar product of Roman decorative sculpture. The Etruscans were already experts in the making of larger terracotta slabs, and the Romans inherited this art from them. In ancient times antefixa were chiefly made of terracotta (P. 65, 111), as well as later on relief-slabs for cymae, for facing wooden beams, etc. Of course the artistic motif corresponds to the Roman taste, although in many cases Greek models were employed, as with the groups of two figures depicting mythological and epic scenes, *e.g.* those represented on the metopes. Thus we see the deeds of Hercules: slaying the lion (P. 84), capturing the bull (P. 85); or Orestes is represented taking refuge on the Omphalos in Apollo's sanctuary

(P. 90). To avoid any misunderstanding, the name of Orestes is scratched in the clay on the right of the hero's head. The terracottas are very sparing of ornamental details. A band of encircled palmettes or palmettes alternating with masks (P. 90) embellished their lower edges (Pp. 84, 85). Other terracottas in which, it is true, the ornamental figures predominate, are more lavishly embellished (*cf.* for instance the terracotta with the figure of Demeter — P. 94). A particularly fine piece of work is a relief with exuberant ornamentation as shown on P. 83[2]: a finely traced acanthus chalice, from which slim scroll ornaments rise, forms a central decorative motif flanked on either side by a girl in a diaphanous garment sitting on the broad leaf of an acanthus chalice. Genre scenes are also favoured, usually of a very picturesque character, and often tinged with humour. A popular theme is the gathering of the grape and pressing out the juice (P. 86[1]): two bearded satyrs, whose sole garment is a skin worn over the shoulder, sit on either side of a vine busily engaged in picking grapes and filling baskets. The next scene depicts two youthful satyrs pressing the juice out of the grapes with their feet (P. 87).

During the last centuries of the Roman Empire the Eastern provinces, where building operations were very extensive (Pp. 115, 116), contributed greatly to the development of sculptural decoration, and produced strikingly picturesque works, the most delicate examples of which are the ornamentations on the M'shatta façade (P. 124—126).

* * *

Early Christian and Byzantine

With the new faith, Christianity, not only another creed was added to the numerous existing religions, but quite a novel spirit was introduced into the world. Antique Hellenic art and that of the Roman Empire harmonized so little with the new *Weltanschauung* and the changed attitude towards all problems of life that there was a great deviation in the whole development of art within the sphere of Graeco⸗Roman culture. But this marked change was not tantamount to a sudden revulsion from the totality of the antique. Definite forms which had obtained for a millennium could not be completely swept away. Nor was it possible to replace the antique technique and numerous antique motifs. Hence the new art developed slowly from the antique by adopting and translating prevailing motifs, re⸗interpreting and then slowly modifying them in accordance with the spirit of the age and the new religion.

Early Christian art is not at first occupied with architecture, but with ornamenting sarcophagi and sepulchres. However, when churches were built, the co⸗operation of decorative sculpture was soon required. The early Christian monumental edifice, the basilica, favoured the arch as a tectonic member, hence a modification of the capitals was necessary, as the springing of the arch was of such a width that the upper surface of the capital was too small. It was therefore imperative to enlarge the abacus. At first a part of the ancient entablature — consisting of architrave, frieze, and cornice — was inserted between the capital and the springing of the arch. This was particulary the case with columns placed in immediate juxtaposition (so⸗called coupled columns). Later on the entablature is replaced by a new member, the dosseret, a square block with sloping sides forming the connecting link between the capital⸗proper and the springing of the arch. In its inception the dosseret had plain surfaces; in the 5th century it was ornamented. In the 6th century, after being completely accommodated to the capital, it was amalgamated with the same.

The dosseret pure and simple is unmistakable (Pp. 138[2], 139), even if some examples are slightly curved (P. 147[4]). The ornamental motifs are allied to those of the abacus *(vide infra)*. The sides (P. 139), or sides and edges, (P. 147[4]) are covered with pierced ornament or leafage.

Birds and animals are also employed as ornamentation on the capitals, as well as scroll⸗work and leafage. The imperial eagle and the ram's head replace the angle volutes. Later on peacocks, cocks, lions, and fabulous monsters were favoured.

The spandrels, walls, ceilings etc. were only ornamented with paintings and mosaic⸗work because Christian art endeavoured to depict symbols and Biblical scenes rather than mere decorative forms. For this reason sculptural art was afforded but little scope. But it asserted itself on the ornamental panels, which are either pierced or embellished with reliefs. These ornamental panels were employed in various ways: as choir-screens, balustrades, and parapets; as windows, and walls surrounding wells. They served also to face pulpits, sarcophagi, etc. The geometrical ornament was revived, and as many motifs had long been regarded as symbols averting evil they were naturally congenial to Christian ideas. Such symbolical patterns were: rosettes, the sun and cross motif, the twirled rosette (P. 146[2]), and the hexagonal star of Istar. These symbolical signs were framed with various patterns such as cable-moulding (P. 150[3]), single (Pp. 128[2], 150[4]) or double (P. 156[2]) and nebule bands with studs. When these bands are more exuberantly decorated the studs are replaced by large circles containing rosettes or also figures (P. 133). Mat-work bands (P. 143, 146, 157) or chain-moulding, the latter consisting of single links (P. 157) or interlaced (P. 129[3]) are also favoured. The spiral ornament (Pp. 150[2], 157), sometimes double (P. 158[1]), is also often met with.

When panels are ornamented with geometrical figures, hexagonal, lozenge, and meander patterns predominate. Crosses are formed of octagons and squares. The symbol of the Cross also occurs in the meander motif, and thus the peculiar T-pattern was evolved (P. 154[1]). It survived for some time as an Islamic ornament.

The floral ornament was also conventionalized under the influence of geometrical patterns which made for severe and rigid contours. Leafage and scroll ornament lose all similitude to nature (P. 134), but the purity and clarity of outline is improved (Pp. 138, 139, 148, 158).

The acanthus undergoes the greatest change. The leaf becomes pointed, sharp and indented. The lobes develop into independent scroll ornament (P. 139[1]) or other complicated patterns (Pp. 133, 139, 147[4]). Sometimes the pattern is so far removed from the antique that it is difficult to recognize the acanthus in its new form.

Ornamental figures were sparsely employed, and only those of a symbolical character were retained. These were, in addition to the symbolic animals of the Evangelists (P. 152), above all eagles (P. 130), pigeons (P. 140), owls (P. 149[1]), and peacocks (Pp. 143, 144), lions (P. 155) or griffins (P. 160), usually depicted in pairs in symetrical heraldic postures. Early Christian art did not favour the representation of the human figure to the extent that Greek art did. For the Greek artist there was no model more perfect than the human body. In spite, however, of what has been said above, early Christian sculptors copied some of the antique types: Cupids, Tritons, Nereides, Pans (P. 149[2]), Menads, etc., as well as mythical scenes. Human figures are only met with in great numbers on sarcophagi and ivories.

* * *

Romanesque

It is natural that the influence of the antique endured for centuries in the Latin countries. But the troubled times, the general impoverishment, and the decay of culture resulted in a marked decline of technical skill. At the same time artistic conceptions and the sense of balance were all but lost. Lowered standards of beauty resulted from a general lack of taste. Another factor was that the cheerful and bright ideas expressed in antique art were not congenial to the mystic, religious, and ascetic conceptions of the new era. It was only towards the middle of the 12th century that architectural and sculptural forms became freer in design and serener in conception. Beauty and grace again found favour and, indeed, were things to be aspired to.

Architecture was always the leading branch of Romanesque art, and this was particulary the case with sacred edifices.

The exterior of the early buildings was not ornamented. In the interior the walls of the nave and aisles were supported by alternating cylindrical and square columns. At first the columns presented little that was novel. The single column was later on replaced by the pier, sometimes composed of numerous separate shafts. At a still later period, when ornament was much more lavishly employed, the shaft was embellished with plastic leafage and mat-work covering the whole surface. The geometrical patterns are simple (P. 186, 187), the stylicised foliage motif (P. 168) is richer. Human figures and all sorts of creatures such as birds and fabulous animals are inserted between the leafage (P. 171).

Romanesque capitals are partly akin to those of the Roman order, especially in countries where a pronounced antique tradition obtained. The Corinthian bell-shaped capital, and especially the composite capital, was much favoured. But there was often a lack of technique in the Corinthian capital (P. 166) The leaves were not infrequently rudely carved, and betrayed little evidence of mastery in design. The clumsy acanthus leaves were more or less bulb-shaped (P. 166). There was little grace in the volutes. Leaves were frequently broad and stunted to the extent that it was difficult to recognize the original pattern (P. 170, 173). Sometimes the conventionalized leaves of other plants were copied in order to augment the decorative effect of the capitals.

The abacus is usually without ornament. But there are also examples of richly decorated capitals; even the abacus and the superimposed architectural members are completely covered with ornament, and so many decorative details are added to the capital to augment the purely picturesque effect that the original bell-shape can hardly be traced. At this period figure motifs become conspicuous. The vertical scroll-work is replaced by eagles of which, in the earlier examples, the heads serve as supports. Although the eagle does not feed on berries, it is often represented picking them from the eye of the volute (P. 170). Usually, however, birds as well as animals are merely inserted in the leafage of the capital for purely decorative purposes without having a special function allotted to them (P. 164), and they are often stylicised in a most fantastic manner. An order of Romanesque capital is the so-called cushion-capital. It is produced by cutting four flat facets out of a bulging circular moulding so as to form a quadrant section on its upper surface (P. 163). This shape supplies the transition from the round column to the square impost supporting the springing of the arch. In order to enlarge the impost a sloping member, the dosseret, is placed over the capital-proper. In its earlier phases the cushion capital is only ornamented with plain leafage or sometimes with figure motifs on the semi-circular facets.

At a later period the flat surfaces were no longer emphasized by ornament, but the whole surface of the cushion-capital was treated as a unit and decorated accordingly with band ornament enriched by leafage (P. 164) and rows of palmettes, etc. The predilection for figure motifs obtained again and the eagles, to take one example, were squeezed into a narrow space, the band ornament was enlivened with serpents' heads and emerged from the mouth of a mask (P. 167).

The ornamentation of Romanesque outer walls is limited at first to the doorways and windows. The deeply recessed (P. 174, 175) and many-moulded portals developed from the necessity to carry an arch over the wide entrance. The mouldings around the windows originated in the same manner. The decorative details of the doorways were at first purely Romanesque. Geometrical patterns: zig-zag ornament, plain diaper, angular rosettes, etc. (P. 186) were favoured on brick edifices in accordance with the limitations of the material. Later on they were transferred to stone buildings (P. 183). These simple motifs are afterwards replaced by leafage ornament. In those countries where the classical tradition still lingered on the acanthus was employed, but interpreted in the Romanesque manner, not, however, to such an extent that the original design was obliterated (P. 175). For the rest, other foliage patterns of a marked conventionalized type were much in vogue. Figures again came to the fore, often of a fantastic or humorous character. Human figures are numerous and, grouped in rows over one or more of the arch-moulds (P. 178), or they are placed (nearly life-size) between and before the jamb-shafts. The larger Romanesque sculptural figures are characterized by their tall, emaciated, famished bodies and ascetic faces in conformity with the spirit of the age which regarded with disfavour a healthy, agile, and powerful frame.

The semicircular slab inserted in the arch is also embellished with simple ornament (P. 174), figure motifs (P. 184), or with fabulous creatures, some of which are pronouncedly decorative (P. 188).

Relief slabs of a similar character were employed to ornament pulpits, lecterns, episcopal thrones, Paschal candelabra, choir-screens, etc. They are either carved in alto-relief, pierced, or nearly so (P. 165). They betray the classic model both in the design of the leaves and scrolls, as well as in composition (P. 169). They show us very clearly what the Romanesque artists had learnt and were finally able to produce in the way of decorative sculpture.

* * *

Gothic

At first ornamental sculpture played but a small rôle in Gothic architecture. Owing to the many profiled members such as the round and square columns, arches, ribs, etc., the interior of the edifice was already so diversified that plastic ornament was not able to assert itself; and had it been able to do so it would have destroyed the balance of the building. The round and square columns which, together with the springing of the vaulting ribs, emphasized the soaring vertical line did not require capitals to exercise their functions. Hence they are simple and comparatively small. Nevertheless, the ornamentation on the bell of the capital is usually of excellent quality, graceful in contour, original in design, and variegated in form. Gothic art chiefly employs on its capitals leafage representing specimens of native plants. Early Gothic capitals were inspired by the Corinthian capital with its supporting angle volutes (P. 203). With the development of the Gothic style the carved foliage appears to be applied to or wrapped round the bell of the capital which is no longer a constructional member, but an ornament. The pronounced plastic treatment of the foliage with its bold undercutting, enhanced by staining the background black or dark-brown, serves to further emphasize the natural appearance of the floral forms in stone (Pp. 217—219).

The details of the foliage ornament, such as the stalks, the dentated edges of the leaves and the ribs are thoroughly naturalistic. Early Gothic art favoured broad, lobated, succulent leaves of swamp and meadow plants. In a later period the artist copied the pointed and dentated leaves of the maple, elm, holly, ivy parsley, marsh-marigold, thistle, etc. Among the older traditional forms to be retained in Gothic ornament were vine-leaves with their effective and beautiful contours, as well as oak leaves interspersed with acorns.

The form of the capitals together with their ornaments are transferred to the corbels (P. 216). They terminate below as a flower or rosette of naturalistic leafage, and sometimes as animal or human heads. In many cases the corbel reproduces a complete human figure.

The exterior of a Gothic edifice affords more scope for plastic ornament than does the interior, and such ornament is always in perfect harmony with the architectural members. The enormous area of the windows, beautifully effective from the interior with their stained glass, was divided up by tracery, continually variegating the pointed arch motif with trefoils and quatrefoils in the heads, as well as roses and rosettes to produce a picturesque effect from the outside. The gables, embellished with blind tracery, the crockets at the angles of the pediments, etc., the finials crowning the perpendicular members, the gablets, balustrades, pinnacles, and the tabernacles, all of an extremely ornate character, together with the figure ornaments, are the distinguishing external decorative traits of Gothic architecture.

The Gothic portal is still more richly decorated with plastic ornament. The recesses are embellished with columns and figures. Seated figures, busts (P. 224), winged angels' heads, as well as grotesque faces and masks throng the casements (P. 205). Scenes from the New Testament are often represented on the tympanum slab: Christ as the Judge of mankind, Mary nursing Jesus, and others.

The Gothic statue only serves decorative purposes, whereas Egyptian plastic art was of symbolic signification, Early Christian Byzantine mystical, Near Eastern laudatory, and Greek an object in itself. Even when Greek plastic art is an auxiliary to architecture it retains its individual and independent traits. Its style is in no way connected with that of the temple, and it is by no means a subordinated member. Now Gothic figures are not conceived as such independent works of art, with perhaps the exception of those on the tympanum, they are only part of a whole, merely ornaments, and are subordinated to the architectural requirements of the edifice (P. 221). Gothic statues were placed in the façade galleries, on the pinnacles, in the tabernacles of the buttresses, in the portal recesses, or in front of the columns in the nave. Their position not only required the perpendicular line to be emphasized, but that the sculptor should be under certain restrictions as to the bearing and attitude of his figures. Hence gesticulation was restrained and the face alone afforded unrestricted scope for interpretation of individual features and expression. And herein lies the great forte of Gothic plastic art. The heads are mostly of high artistic quality (Pp. 208, 210, 211).

The artist's imagination and ingenuity is best perceived in the grotesque figures of animals and monsters employed as gargoyles (P. 223), or carved as reliefs on the portal frieze (P. 223), balustrades (P. 204), percloses, and on the stalls, where they were most exuberant. It is true that many of these figures are highly burlesque, and of ribald humour, but this was in accordance with the spirit of the period. The desired decorative effect was not always fully attained to owing on the one hand to the unfavourable position in which the statues were placed (usually at a considerable height), and on the other to the superabundance of ornamental features surrounding them. However, we should remember that the statues were brightly coloured, especially the garments, and that gilding was also often resorted to. There can be little doubt that, owing to their many colours, they served their purpose as integral members of the whole. Though they have lost their hues, they still contribute largely to the imposing effect of Gothic edifices.

* * *

The Renaissance

In those countries where classic traditions obtained and had not been modified by a new art movement (as for instance in the Byzantine and Islamic countries), antique art never ceased to exercise its rejuvenating and ennobling influence. For this reason it is not correct to speak of the Renaissance as a new birth of antique art, aside from the fact that such a revival or imitation was not intended by the creators and great masters of this period. Thus the Renaissance is not an attempt to revive the antique, nor is it a conscious continuation on the part of its creators.

It cannot of course be denied that the Renaissance owes much to the antique. Nevertheless, Renaissance art always followed its own bent. Renaissance architects were not influenced by the tectonic principles obtaining in antique monumental edifices. At first they only borrowed decorative details to a greater extent than did their predecessors. Later on, however, tectonic details were more closely adhered to. And when antique decorative motifs and ornament were drawn from it appears to have been done at the outset without any comprehension of their inherent qualities. In after years Greek and Roman remains were carefully studied, and a selection made from the wealth of antique motifs in accordance with the taste of the artist.

The Renaissance architects, it is true, adopted the original orders of the columns, but they endeavoured to breathe new life into them in the same manner as the classic architect varied the order of the columns to suit his personal taste.

The Doric-Tuscan column in its austere simplicity did not appeal to the exuberant taste for ornament favoured by the architects of the Renaissance. But where it is employed, as for instance in the courtyard of the Cancelleria in Rome by Bramante, this order is also richly decorated. A leafage wreath and frieze of rosettes separated by a matted band surround the neck; the echinus is ornamented with leafage scrolls. When the Ionic capital is employed it either adheres closely to the antique model or is lavishly ornamented: the volutes are embellished with leaves, among which figures are sometimes inserted, the elongated neck is wrapped in acanthus leaves. Michelangelo designed a more luxuriant form for the Capitoline buildings with little festoons between the eyes of the volutes and lion's masks on the abacus.

The Corinthian composite capital appealed to the Renaissance architects because of its greater wealth of ornament, especially as they were familiar with many ornate examples dating from the period of the Roman Empire. The ornamented neck of the column is encircled by an echinus, much akin to the Doric, with large egg and tongue and small bead moulding from which the four volutes spring with leafage drooping well below the echinus. Another motif is a bell-shaped capital with figure or foliage ornament and sometimes embellished with angle volutes (P. 249). The plastic ornament of these composite capitals is usually very delicate and much diversified. In addition to the floral ornament, conventionalized human figures (Pp. 249, 256), heads, sphinxes, animals, winged-horses, dolphins (P. 250), cornucopiae and vases with flowers and fruit (P. 251), masks, coats of arms, emblems (P. 247), etc. were usually employed as decorative ornament and grouped in fantastic patterns. The capitals of the square columns and pilasters were treated in the same manner (P. 265), and their ornament was often carried onto the entablature.

The so-called candelabrum-columns rest on ornamental pedestals and spring from an exuberant chalice of leaves forming the base. The round shaft, festooned with garlands or completely covered with decorative motifs, supports a Corinthian composite capital. The candelabrum-columns are used as supports, or are placed in front of portals and monuments in the form of half columns or pilasters.

Sometimes the pilasters are ornamented in the same manner as the columns, or each face is differently decorated. They are framed with bead moulding, ribbon-work, etc. and the panel is filled with leafage and scroll ornament issuing from richly decorated vases; graceful figures are often inserted in the foliage (P. 240, 241). It would appear that the Renaissance architect attached particular value to the designing and treatment of such ornamental panels. Just this type of ornament displays a most vivid imagination and an inimitable grace. Very often atlantes and caryatides, and sometimes busts terminating in ornamental patterns serve as supports. In many cases the caryatides are placed in front of pilasters or window and door jambs merely as decorative members, but in such a manner as to suggest supports when seen from below; however, animals and fabulous monsters not infrequently replace human figures as architectural supports. Indeed, Renaissance art devotes much attention to figure motifs, but employs them quite differently from Gothic art. Doubtlessly the predilection for figure ornament is partly due to the fact that numerous architects were also sculptors, and that sculptural art in the erly days of the Renaissance was well ahead of its sister branches. The sculptor was the first to turn his attention to classic models, and had not only acquired a certain amount of skill in composition, but had also become an adept in the portrayal of the human figure and drapery as, *inter alia,* is shown in the works of Andrea Pisano (1273—1349), (Pp. 236—239), or in the figures on Sta. Maria dei Fiore in Florence whose drapery is of antique simplicity though dating from the beginning of the 14th century.

It was of great advantage to decorative sculpture of that period that the greatest sculptors also helped to adorn the edifices themselves, and, in fact, most of their work was destined for decorative purposes in contradistinction to that of the ancient Egyptian artists. One result was the close connection between architecture and sculpture. They both seem to contribute equally to the effect of an inseparable whole and are so well balanced that, as for instance with Donatello's pulpit in S. Croce in Florence, the plastic details do not appear to be subordinate members of the architecture. Donatello's reliefs for the singing gallery illustrate very clearly the relationship between the Renaissance artist and classic art. There is hardly a detail that has not been borrowed from antique models, and yet the impression of the whole is distinctly suggestive of the Renaissance spirit, than which nothing is less antique. Although the artist follows antique models he imbues his work with a spirit of his own and creates something possessing quite an independent character.

* * *

Islamic Art

Wherever the Mohammedan set foot he found an ancient culture and an autochthonous art which of course differed in the various countries.

Islamic monumental edifices are simple in plan. Mosques, schools, palaces, caravansaries, etc. are all of similar architectural disposition. The leading features are an enclosed square, columned halls, and arcades with closed apartments behind.

The interior of Saracenic buildings is exuberantly decorated. At the outset of Islamic art, antique, Early Christian and Byzantine columns were employed indiscriminately, and it was some time before a specifically Mohammedan order was evolved.

The Islamic-Saracenic column consists of a long slender shaft, astragals, a long leafage-wrapped neck, and a capital with a convex outline richly decorated with arabesques (P. 317). The Osmanic column is of more recent date and has a stalactite or invected capital. The various forms of the arches, as well as of the vaults, are also decorated with stalactite ornament (Pp. 315, 318). This ornament is formed of a number of successive layers of small niches starting from a series of brackets, each row projecting beyond the row below it. And the stalactite motif is often employed to decorate spandrels and door or window jambs (Pp. 310, 311, 314, 315, 318).

Surface ornament and wall decoration have their sources in the motifs of the various countries and periods which, however, the Mohammedan artist skilfully combined to form a new style. Geometrical patterns of all sorts, consisting of straight, waved, curved and other lines are worked into elaborate interlacing, often connected with beautiful conventional floral ornament. This conventional floral ornament (called arabesques) is one of the main features of Arabic decorative art and has become indispensable and permanent as an ornamental motif. Leaves, blossoms and fruit, which are stylicised in a peculiar manner, are of common occurrence, as well as conventionalized grotesque animals, and sometimes even human figures. Arabic letters, which are extremely picturesque (Pp. 302—318), were well adapted for decorative motifs and thus proverbs and texts from the Koran were frequently interwoven in the patterns. It will be remembered that the ancient Egyptians also used their hieroglyphs as decorative motifs.

This wealth of motifs was combined to form the richest and most exuberant patterns and to cover every surface requiring ornament, and during the most flourishing period of Islamic culture practically every imaginable surface was ornamented. Surface ornament was largely employed on ceramics, illuminated parchments, wood carvings, ivories, embossed leather, inlay-work, incised metal (arms), fabrics, carpets and on other products of arts and crafts.

In Europe Islamic art attained to great perfection in Sicily and particularly in Spain. Above all those remarkable capitals with their basket-work tracery (P. 320) of the synagogue (now Santa Maria la Blanca) in Toledo erected in the 13th and 14th centuries show how independently Moorish art developed in Spain without losing its Islamic features.

The culminating point of Islamic architecture in the western part of the Mohammedan world is doubtlessly the magnificent Castle of the Alhambra — which received its name from its reddish stones. In its exuberant fancy Moorish style comes to its climax. It was erected in the 13th and 14th centuries and consists of several palaces connected with each other. The exterior presents the appearance of a mountain stronghold of a solid architectural character which hardly permits one to guess at the beauties of the interior. Here is a series of courtyards and halls displaying all the richness and delicacy which the Moorish artist was able to conceive. The halls and courtyards were connected by large richly ornamented arches which could only be closed by means of carpets, as doors were seldom employed. The numerous columns, sometimes in groups of twos and fours, with broad neck rings and capitals embedded in exuberant leafage, support the most varied types of arches richly ornamented with stalactites and hanging work (Pp. 314—317). All these architectural details, together with the arabesques interwoven with letter ornament covering the surfaces of the walls (P. 313) are wondrously beautiful in their decorative effect. It is evident that Islamic art had attained to its highest aim which had always been the perfection of ornament and embellishment.

* * *

The following is a list of plates giving the places and names of the museums in which the originals can le found:

Athens, National Museum Plates 40, 41, 47, 48, 50, 52, 58, 61, 78, 79.

Berlin, State Museums: Antique Section Plates 34, 35, 37, 45, 54, 55, 59, 60, 62. Egyptian Section Plates 2, 3, 5, 6, 8, 9, 11, 13. Kaiser-Friedrich-Museum Plates 124, 125, 126, 128, 129, 131, 132, 134, 137, 150, 151, 154, 155, 290, 297, 300, 301.

Boston, Museum of Fine Art Plates 49.

Florence, National Museum Plates 7, 11, 68, 298, 299.

Cairo, Museum Plates 1, 133.

London, British Museum Plates 21, 22, 23, 24, 25, 26, 27, 28, 41, 49, 56, 57.

New York, Metropolitan Museum of Art Plates 32, 33, 134.

Paris, Louvre Museum Plates 7, 14, 15, 16, 20, 29, 36, 38, 42, 44, 64, 68, 77, 102.

Rome, Capitol Museum Plates 73, 107, Lateran Plates 86, 97, 101, 108, 109, National Museum Plates 51, 53, 71, 72, 81, 82, 86, 103, 107, 110, Vatican Plates 65, 71, 76, 84, 85, 87, 90, 98, 104, 122, Villa Giulia Plates 83, 91, 111.

List of plates reproduced from photographs supplied by the fellowing publichers:

Alinari, Florence
Plates 7, 10, 11, 40, 41, 48, 50, 51, 52, 58, 61, 63, 65, 68, 71, 73, 78, 79, 81, 82, 84, 85, 86, 90, 97, 103, 107–112, 117, 136–147, 149, 151, 170, 171, 196, 236–248, 250–254, 259–263, 265, 298, 299.

Brogi, Florence
Plates 43, 53, 82, 86, 91, 168, 256.

Coolidge, Baldwin, Boston
Plates 49.

Giraudon, A., Paris
Plates 14, 15, 20, 29, 36, 38, 42, 44, 64, 68, 77, 164, 173, 192, 195, 208, 209–212.

Laurent y Cia, Madrid
Plates 312–318.

Mansell, W. F., Elfin Works
Plates 21, 22, 23, 24, 25, 27, 28, 41, 49, 57.

Staatliche Bildstelle, Berlin
Plates 2, 3, 5, 6, 9, 11, 13, 114, 115, 132.

From: "Les Monuments Mauresques du Maroc" (Lévy, Paris)
Plates 309, 310, 311, 319.

From: v. Bissing, "Denkmäler" (Bruckmann, München)
Plates 1, 11, 130.

THE PLATES

EGYPT, ANCIENT EMPIRE — HEAD OF A STATUE OF KING KHAFRA WITH FALCON

EGYPT, MIDDLE EMPIRE — FISHING, LIMESTONE. ABOUT 3000 B. C.

EGYPT, MIDDLE EMPIRE — BOAT IN PAPYRUS THICKET, LIMESTONE RELIEF. ABOUT 3000 B. C.

EGYPT, NEW EMPIRE — RELIEF, INCENSE TREES, FROM THE TEMPLE OF AMON, DEIR EL BAHARI

EGYPT, NEW EMPIRE — RELIEF FROM A KING'S TOMB

EGYPT — DETAILS FROM A FUNERAL PROCESSION, MEMPHIS. ABOUT 1300

1

2

EGYPT — 1. RELIEF FROM THE SARCOPHAGUS OF RAMSES III.
2. PART OF A LIMESTONE RELIEF. XVII CENTURY B. C.

EGYPT, NEW EMPIRE — PART OF WOODEN ANOINTING SPOON

1

2

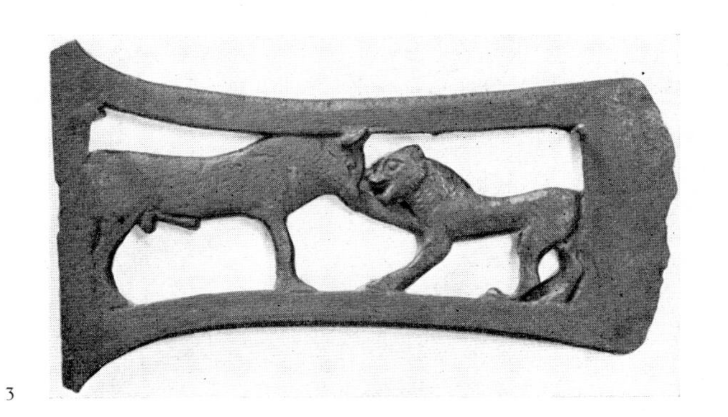

3

4

5

EGYPT — 1.—3. ORNAMENTAL BRONZE AXE BLADES, ABOUT 1400 B.C. 4. RELIEF ON A COSMETIC PALETTE, 4000 B.C. 5. FRAGMENT FROM A TOMB RELIEF, 3000 B.C.

EGYPT, NEW EMPIRE — LIMESTONE SCULPTURE. XV CENTURY B. C.

1

2

EGYPT — 1. LIMESTONE FIGURE OF A WOMAN GRINDING CORN. 2300 B. C.
2. LIMESTONE BOWL WITH FIGURE. 1400 B. C.

EGYPT, NEW EMPIRE — LION AND SPHINX, GRANITE

EGYPT, NEW EMPIRE — 1. SPHINX FROM A STAIRWAY OF DIOCLETIAN'S PALACE, SPALATO
2. RAM FROM A SPHINX AVENUE ERECTED BY AMENOPHIS III.

EGYPT, LATE EMPIRE — WOMAN'S HEAD

MESOPOTAMIA — HEAD OF A STATUE FROM TELLO–LAGASH. ABOUT 2500 B. C.

RELIEF ON A STELE CONTAINING THE LAWS OF HAMMURABI. FROM SUSA
ABOUT 2000 B. C.

BABYLON — STONE TABLET OF KING MARDUKBALIDDIN II. 715 B.C.

BABYLON — BULL AND DRAGON. GLAZED BRICK RELIEFS FROM THE ISHTAR GATE
ABOUT 570 B.C.

1

2

SUSA — 1. WINGED BULL, UNGLAZED BRICK RELIEF. 2. LION FRIEZE COLOURED GLAZED BRICK

ASSYRIAN — RELIEF FROM THE KING'S PALACE IN NINEVAH. VII CENTURY B.C.

ASSYRIAN — ALABASTER RELIEF FROM KUYUNJIK–NINEVAH. VII CENTURY B.C.
LONDON, BRITISH MUSEUM

ASSYRIAN — ALABASTER RELIEFS FROM KUYUNJIK–NINEVAH. VII CENTURY B.C.
LONDON, BRITISH MUSEUM

ASSYRIAN — ALABASTER RELIEFS FROM KUYUNJIK–NINEVAH. VII CENTURY B.C.
LONDON, BRITISH MUSEUM

ASSYRIAN — ALABASTER RELIEF FROM KUYUNJIK–NINEVAH. VII CENTURY B.C.
LONDON, BRITISH MUSEUM

ASSYRIAN — RELIEF FROM THE PALACE OF SENACHERIB IN NINEVAH
VII CENTURY B.C. LONDON, BRITISH MUSEUM

ASSYRIAN — SIEGE OF THE CITY. RELIEF FROM THE TIME OF SENACHERIB. VII CENTURY B.C.
LONDON, BRITISH MUSEUM

ASSYRIAN — FISHING ON THE TIGRIS. RELIEF FROM THE PALACE OF SENACHERIB. VII CENTURY B.C.
LONDON, BRITISH MUSEUM

ASSYRIAN — ARCHITECTURAL FRAGMENT FROM THE PALACE OF SENACHERIB
VII CENTURY B.C. LONDON, BRITISH MUSEUM

1

2

1. COLUMN BASE FROM SUSA. IV CENTURY B. C. 2. HITTITE COLUMN BASE FROM SENDSHIRLI. IX CENTURY B. C.

HITTITE STONE RELIEFS. II CENTURY B. C.

HITTITE STONE RELIEFS. VII CENTURY B.C.

CYPRIOT SARCOPHAGUS. VI CENTURY B.C.

CYPRIAN SARCOPHAGUS. END VIEW. V CENTURY B. C.

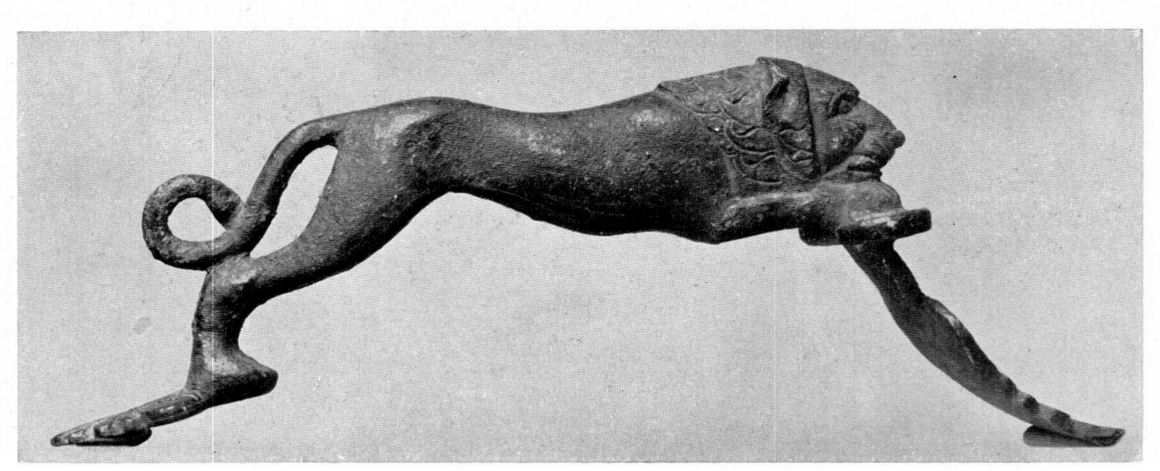

GREEK — VASE DECORATION IN BRONZE. VI CENTURY B.C.

GREEK — DISH IN BRONZE. VI CENTURY B. C.

GREEK — VASE HANDLE AND GRIFFENS IN BRONZE
VII—VI CENTURY B. C.

1

2

3

DECORATION IN BRONZE — 1. AND 2. GREEK, VI CENTURY B. C.
3. ROMAN, V CENTURY B. C.

GREEK — ALTAR RELIEF FROM THE ISLAND OF THASOS. 480. B. C.

GREEK — METOPE FROM THE TEMPLE OF HERA IN SELINUS. MIDDLE OF V CENTURY B.C.

1

2

GREEK — 1. OLD IONIC ANTAE CAPITAL FROM MILET. VI CENTURY B.C.
2. PART OF A FRIEZE FROM THE ERECHTHEION. V CENTURY B.C.

1

2

GREEK — 1. IONIC CAPITAL FROM THE TEMPLE OF ARTEMIS (EPHESOS) 547 B.C.
2. CORINTHIAN CAPITAL FROM POLYCLITUS TEMPLE (EPIDAURUS) IV CENTURY B.C.

GREEK — DETAILS OF ARCHITECTURE FROM THE APOLLON TEMPLE IN MILET
IV CENTURY B. C.

GREEK — PILASTER CAPITAL FROM MEGARA HYBLAEA. END OF VI CENTURY B. C.

GREEK — FRAGMENT OF THE APOLLON TEMPLE IN MILET. IV CENTURY B.C.

GREEK — DETAILS OF ARCHITECTURE AND ALTAR FRAGMENTS. V CENTURY B. C.

1

2

1. GREEK — GABLE AKROTERION FROM THE TEMPLE OF APHAEA (AEGINA) V CENTURY B. C. 2. ROMAN — CORNER AKROTERION FROM THE TRAJAN TEMPLE (PERGAMON) II CENTURY A.D.

GREEK — DECORATIVE VASES IN MARBLE. IV CENTURY B.C.

GREEK — LIONS' HEADS. V CENTURY B. C.

1

2

GREEK — 1. RAM'S HEAD IN MARBLE. IV CENTURY B.C. 2. HORSE'S HEAD FROM THE PEDIMENT OF THE PARTHENON. V CENTURY B.C.

GREEK — SPHINX. V CENTURY B. C.

GREEK — MASKS IN STONE AND TERRA-COTTA. VI—IV CENTURY B. C.

GREEK — PART OF A GRAVE MEMORIAL. V CENTURY B. C.

GREEK — ALTAR RELIEF. V CENTURY B. C.

GREEK — DANCING WOMEN. ATTIC WORK. V CENTURY B. C.

GREEK — VOTIVE RELIEF. V CENTURY B. C.

GREEK — BELLEROPHON AND CHIMAERA. TERRA-COTTA RELIEF. V CENTURY B. C.

GREEK — HORSE-TAMER. MARBLE RELIEF FROM THE VILLA HADRIANI. ROME. V CENTURY B. C.

GREEK — GRAVESTONE. V CENTURY B. C.

GREEK — GRAVESTONE FROM PERGAMON. II CENTURY B. C.

GREEK — GRAVESTONE FROM PERGAMON. II CENTURY B. C.

GREEK — GRAVESTONE. III CENTURY B. C.

HELLENIC — CLAY FIGURES. II CENTURY B. C.

HELLENIC — RELIEF FROM A CINERARY URN. II CENTURY B. C.

MASKS IN BRONZE — GREEK AND ROMAN

ETRUSCAN — ANTE-FIXAE IN TERRA-COTTA. V—IV CENTURY B. C.

MASKS IN STONE AND TERRA-COTTA. GREECE AND ROME
IV—III CENTURY B. C.

MASKS IN STONE AND TERRA-COTTA. GREECE AND ROME
II CENTURY B. C. AND I CENTURY A. D.

ETRUSCAN — FABULOUS ANIMALS IN BRONZE. V CENTURY B. C.

ETRUSCAN — FABULOUS ANIMALS IN BRONZE. V CENTURY B. C.

ETRUSCAN — BRONZE DECORATION. V AND III CENTURY B. C.

1

2

3

BRONZE DECORATION — 1. AND 2. ROMAN, FOUND IN LAKE OF NEMI
3. ROMAN. III CENTURY B. C.

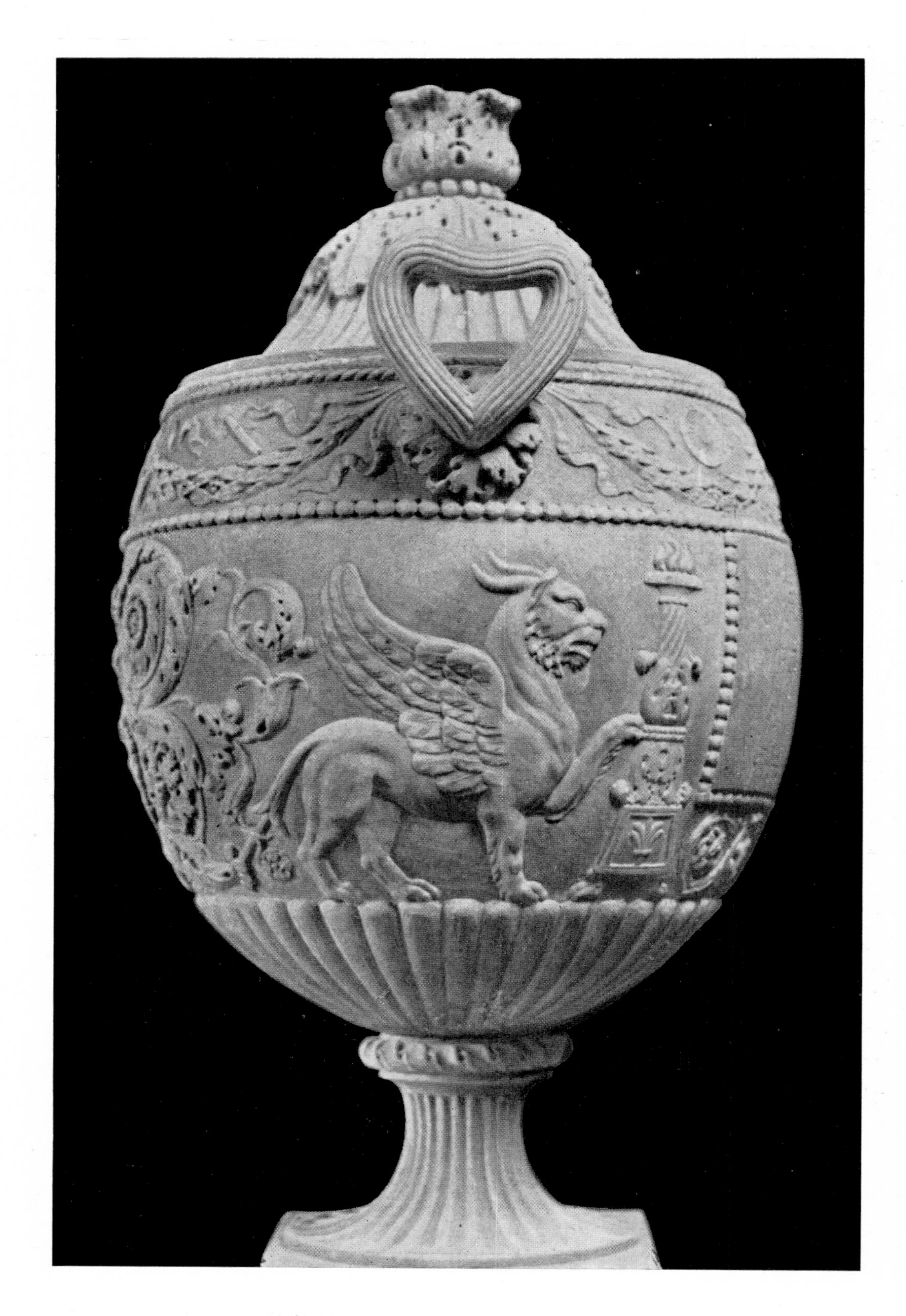

ROMAN CINERARY URN. II CENTURY A. D.

ROMAN VASE IN MARBLE. II CENTURY A. D.

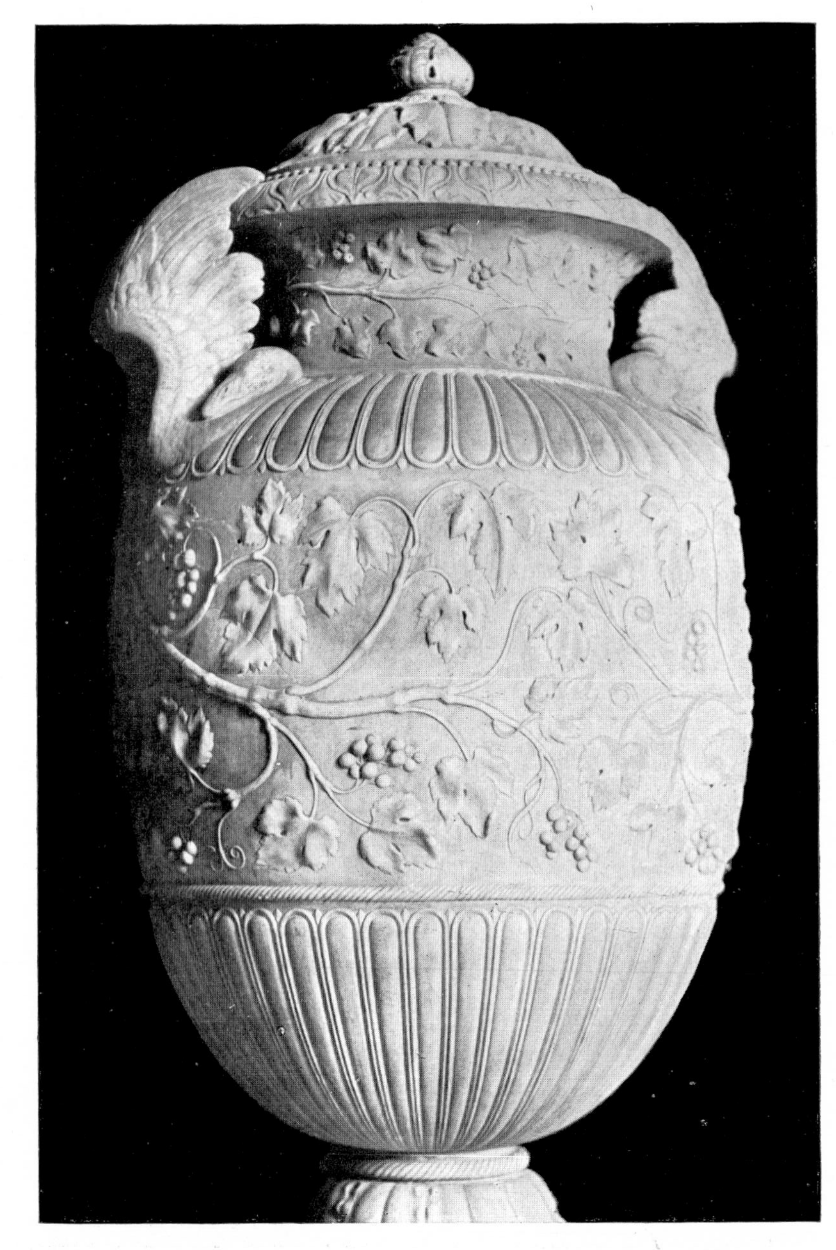

ROMAN CINERARY URNS IN MARBLE. I CENTURY A. D.

ROMAN CINERARY URNS IN MARBLE. I AND II CENTURY A. D.

ROMAN VASES IN MARBLE. I CENTURY A. D.

ROMAN VASES IN MARBLE. I CENTURY A. D.

ROMAN SARCOPHAGUS. I CENTURY A. D.

ROMAN SARCOPHAGUS. I CENTURY A. D.

ROME — RELIEF PLATE. III CENTURY A. D.

ROME — FRAGMENT OF A SARCOPHAGUS. I CENTURY A.D.

1

2

ROMAN — 1. TERRA-COTTA FRIEZE. 2. GARGOYLE. I CENTURY B.C.

ROMAN TERRA-COTTA FRIEZES. I CENTURY A. D.

ROMAN TERRA-COTTA FRIEZE. I CENTURY A. D.

ROMAN TERRA-COTTA FRIEZE. I CENTURY A. D.

ROMAN TERRA-COTTA FRIEZES. I CENTURY A. D.

ROMAN TERRA–COTTA FRIEZES. I CENTURY A.D.

ROMAN — BACCHANALIAN FRIEZE IN MARBLE. I CENTURY A.D.

ROMAN — BACCHANTES. I CENTURY A.D.

ROMAN TERRA–COTTA FRIEZE. I CENTURY A.D.

ROMAN TERRA-COTTA FRIEZE. I CENTURY A.D.

1

2

3

ROMAN RELIEF PLASTIC. I CENTURY A.D. 1. ISIS PROCESSION
2. FRIEZE FROM HERCULANEUM. 3. CORYBANT DANCE

1

2

ROMAN RELIEF PLASTIC. I CENTURY A.D. 1. DIONYSIUS PROCESSION
2. MERCURY, PALLAS, APOLLO

ROMAN TERRA-COTTA FRIEZE. II CENTURY A.D.

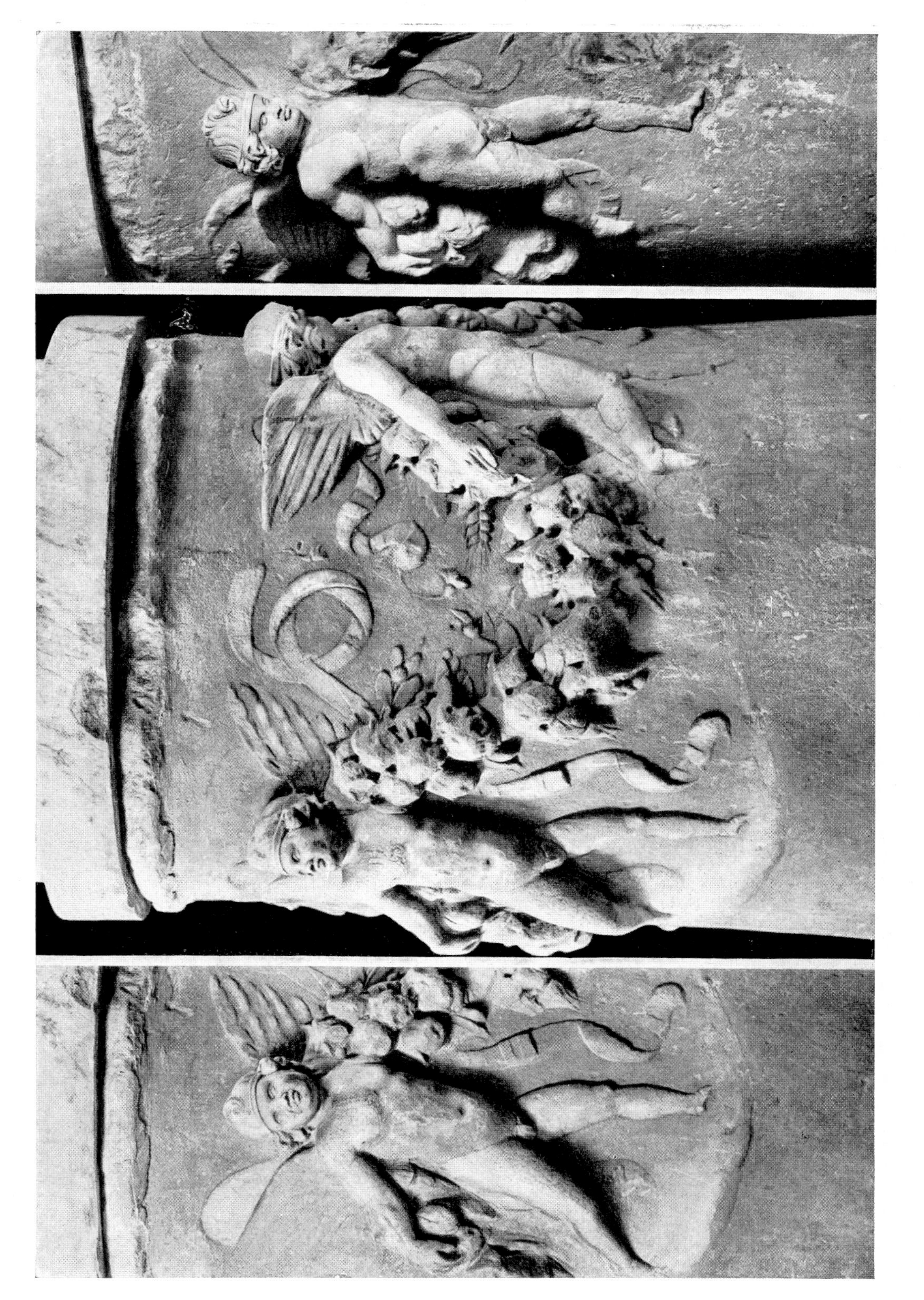

ROMAN — ROUND ALTAR DECORATION. I CENTURY A.D.

ROMAN — PART OF AN ORNAMENT FROM THE FORUM ROMANUM. I CENTURY A.D.

ROMAN — ORNAMENTAL FRIEZES. II CENTURY A. D.

ROMAN — PEACOCK IN BRONZE. I CENTURY A.D.

ROMAN — CARYATIDES IN MARBLE. I CENTURY A.D.

ROMAN — RELIEF IN MARBLE. III CENTURY A. D.

ROMAN — PILASTER DECORATION. I CENTURY A. D.

ROMAN ARM–CHAIR IN MARBLE. I CENTURY A. D.

ROMAN MARBLE TABLE. II CENTURY A. D.

ROMAN — PILASTER DECORATION. II CENTURY A.D.

ROMAN — FRAGMENTS OF DECORATION. II CENTURY A. D.

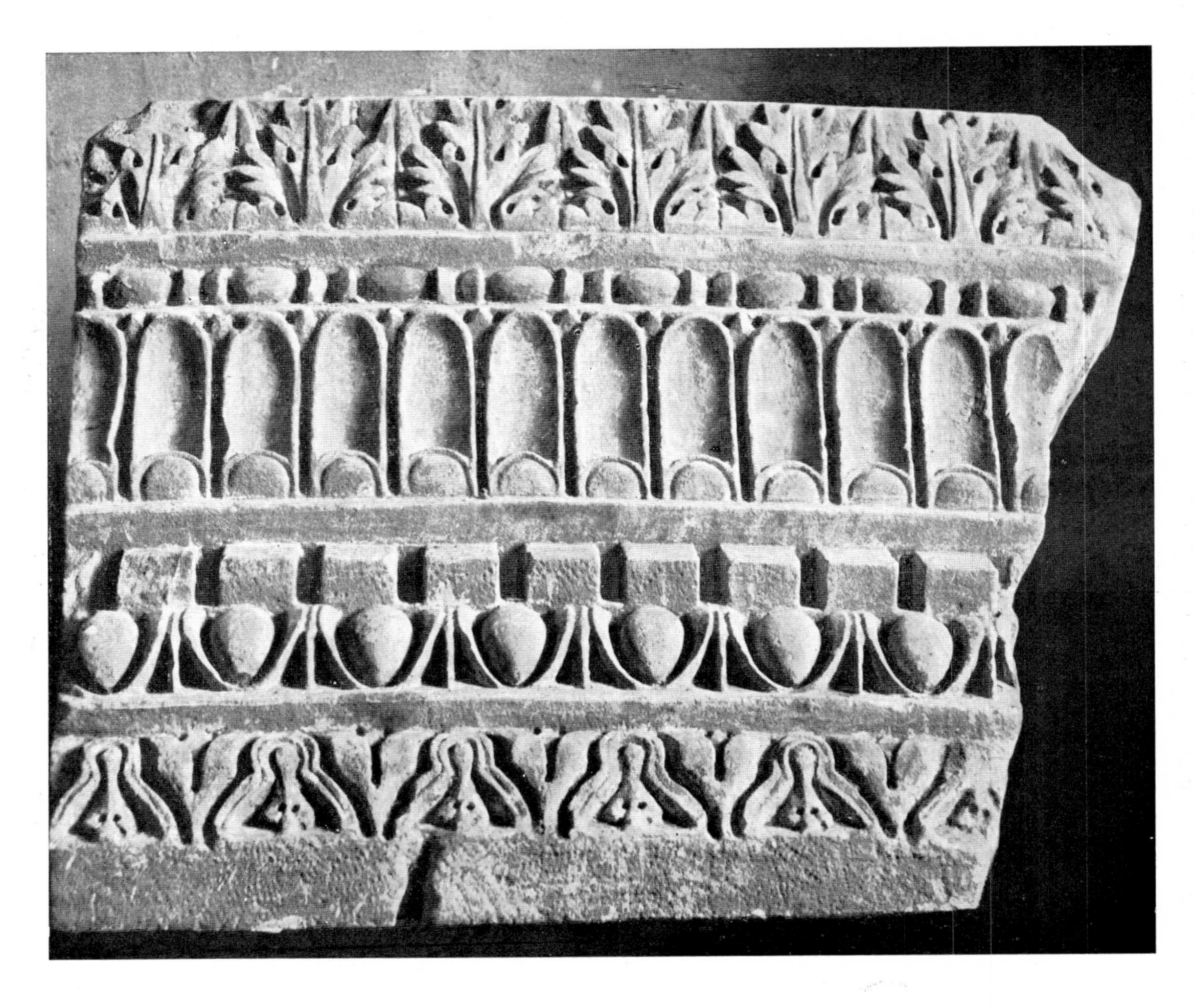

FRAGMENTS OF ROMAN ARCHITECTURE. I AND II CENTURY A. D.

ROMAN — 1. CAPITAL. 2. BASE OF A COLUMN. I CENTURY A. D.

ROMAN CAPITALS. II CENTURY A.D.

ROMAN CAPITALS. I CENTURY A. D.

ROMAN — FRAGMENT OF ARCHITECTURE IN TERRA-COTTA. I CENTURY A.D.

ROMAN ANTE–FIX IN TERRA–COTTA. I CENTURY A. D.

ROMAN — FRAGMENT FROM THE TEMPLE OF VESPASIAN, ROME. 80 A. D.

ROMAN — CEILING IN THE TEMPLE OF JUPITER AT SPALATO
END OF III CENTURY A. D.

ROMAN — FRAGMENTS OF ARCHITECTURE FROM BAALBEK. III CENTURY A. D.

ROMAN — FRAGMENTS OF ARCHITECTURE FROM BAALBEK. III CENTURY A. D.

ROMAN — FRAGMENTS OF DECORATION. II CENTURY A.D.

ROMAN — 1. FRAGMENTS OF CARYATIDES. 2. CAPITALS. III CENTURY A.D.

ROMAN GRAVESTONES. II CENTURY A. D.

ROMAN GRAVESTONE AND DECORATIVE FRIEZE. I CENTURY A.D.

ROMAN GRAVESTONE, II CENTURY A. D.

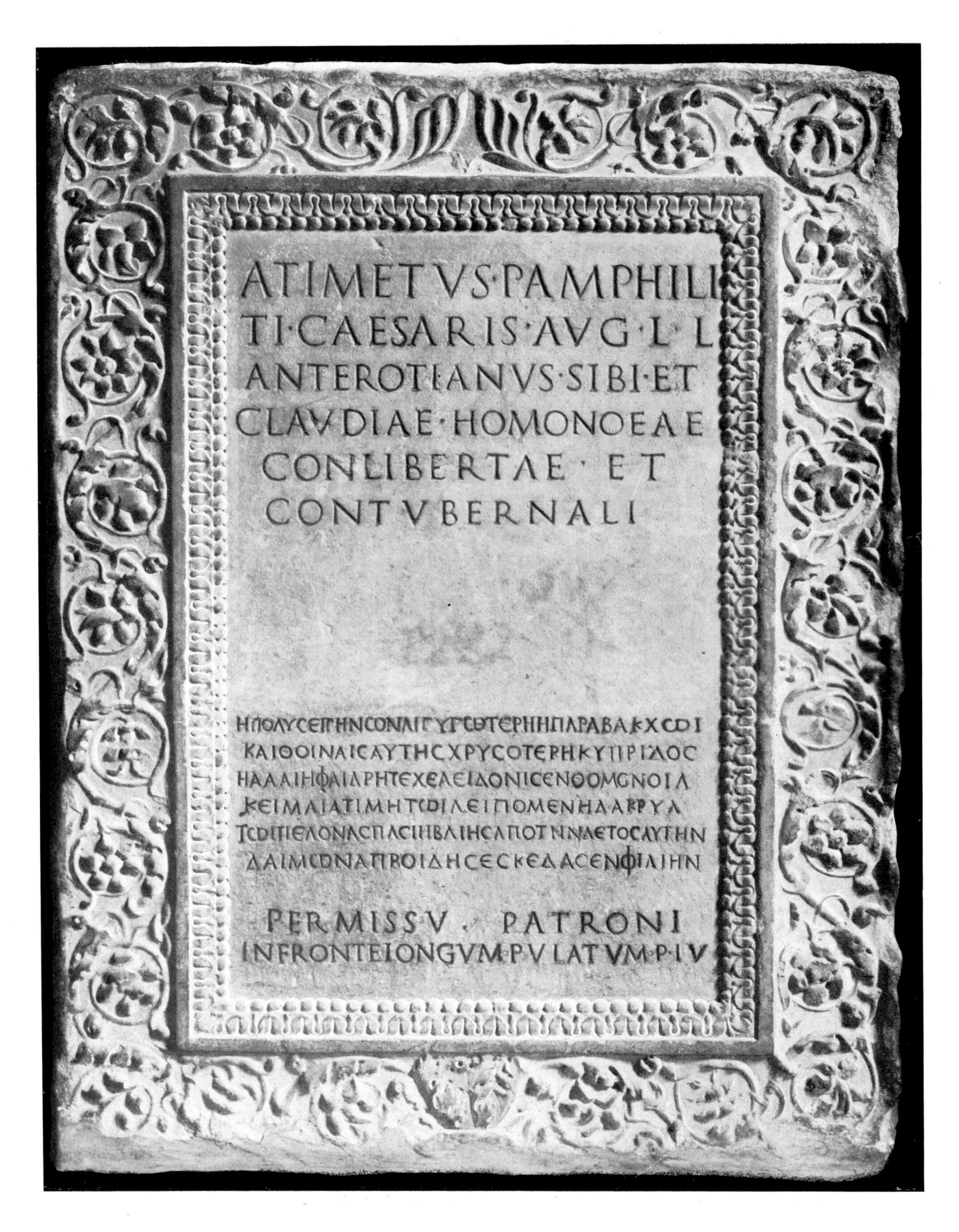

ROMAN GRAVESTONE. II CENTURY A. D.

ROMAN GRAVESTONE. II CENTURY A. D.

1

2

ROMAN — 1. SARCOPHAGUS RELIEF. III CENTURY A.D.
2. LATE-ROMAN GRAVESTONE FROM SALONA (DALMATIA)

SYRIAN — DECORATION FROM THE MSCHATTA FAÇADE. VI CENTURY A.D.

SYRIAN — DECORATION FROM THE MSCHATTA FAÇADE. VI CENTURY A.D.

SYRIAN — DECORATION FROM THE MSCHATTA FAÇADE. VI CENTURY A.D.

SYRIAN — DECORATION FROM THE MSCHATTA FAÇADE

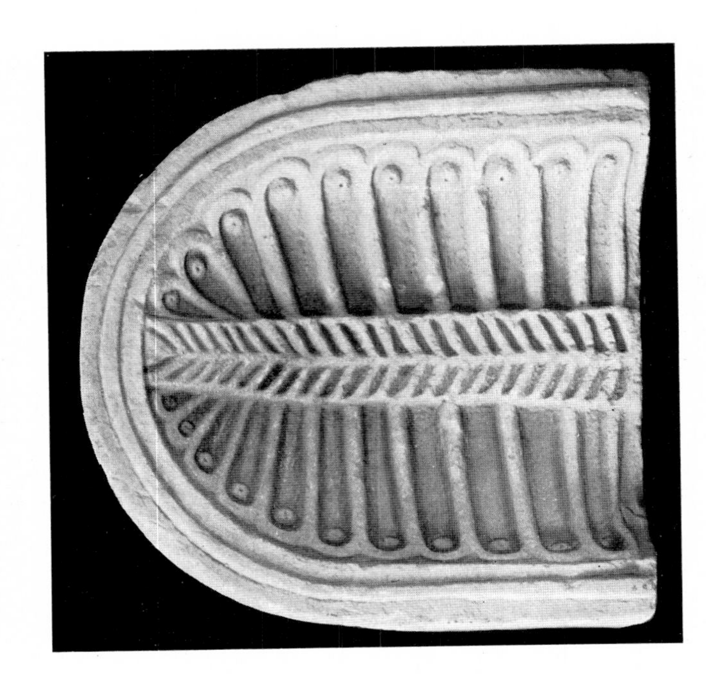

COPTIC — ARCHITECTURE DECORATION IN LIME-STONE. VI CENTURY A.D.

COPTIC — LIME-STONE PILASTER AND DECORATIVE WOOD PANELS. VI—VII CENTURY

COPTIC GRAVESTONE. 700 A. D.

COPTIC — DECORATIVE WOOD PANELS. VI—VII CENTURY

COPTIC — FRIEZES AND DECORATIVE FIGURES IN WOOD. VI CENTURY

1

2

3

COPTIC — 1. AND 2. FRAGMENTS OF ARCHITECTURE IN LIME-STONE
3. DECORATIVE FRIEZE IN WOOD. VI CENTURY

1

2

EARLY-CHRISTIAN — 1. LIME-STONE PEDEDSTAL FROM SYRIA. IX CENTURY A. D.
2. RELIEF PLATE IN LIME-STONE. VII—VIII CENTURY

BYZANTINE CAPITALS. VI CENTURY

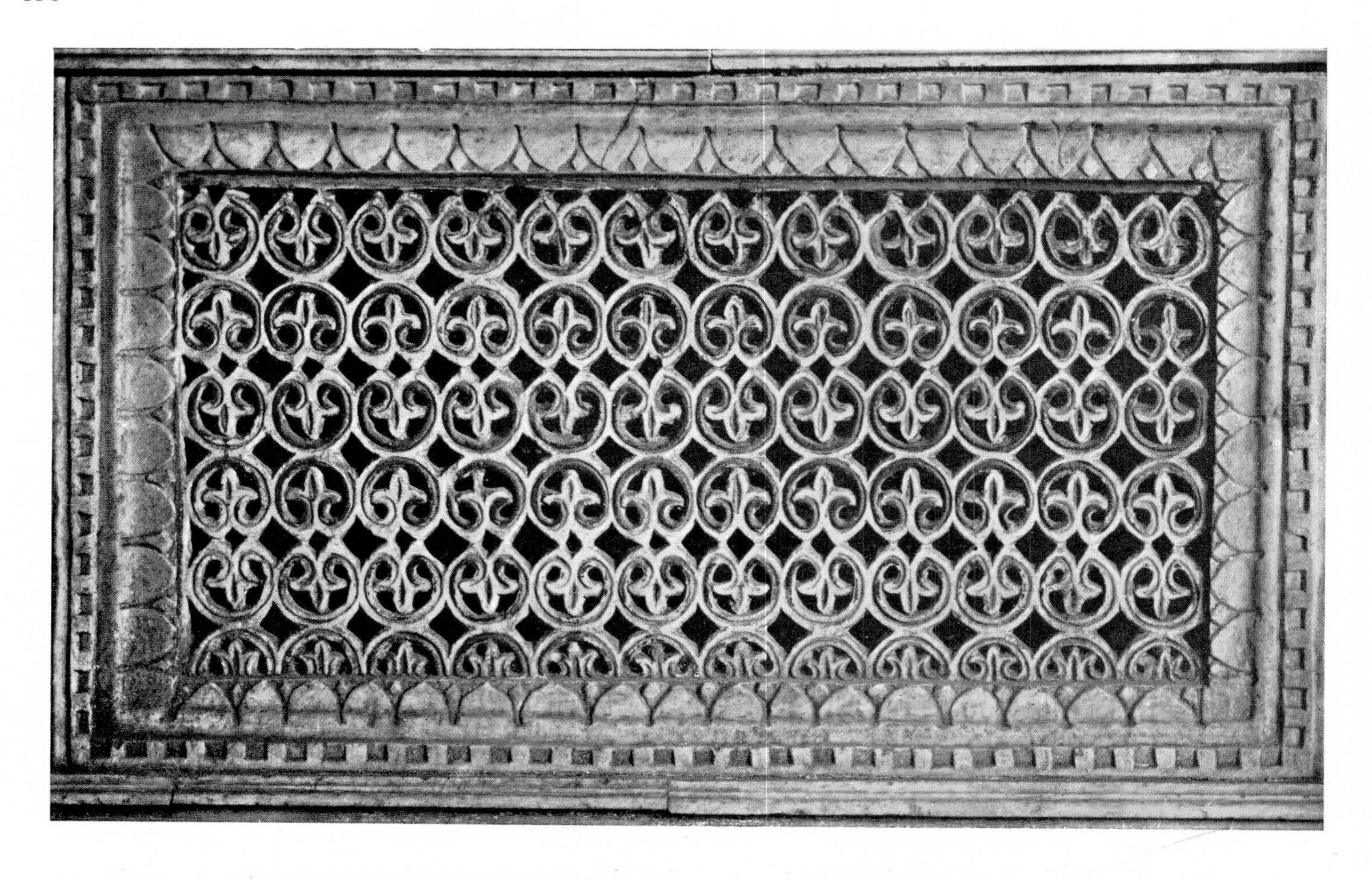

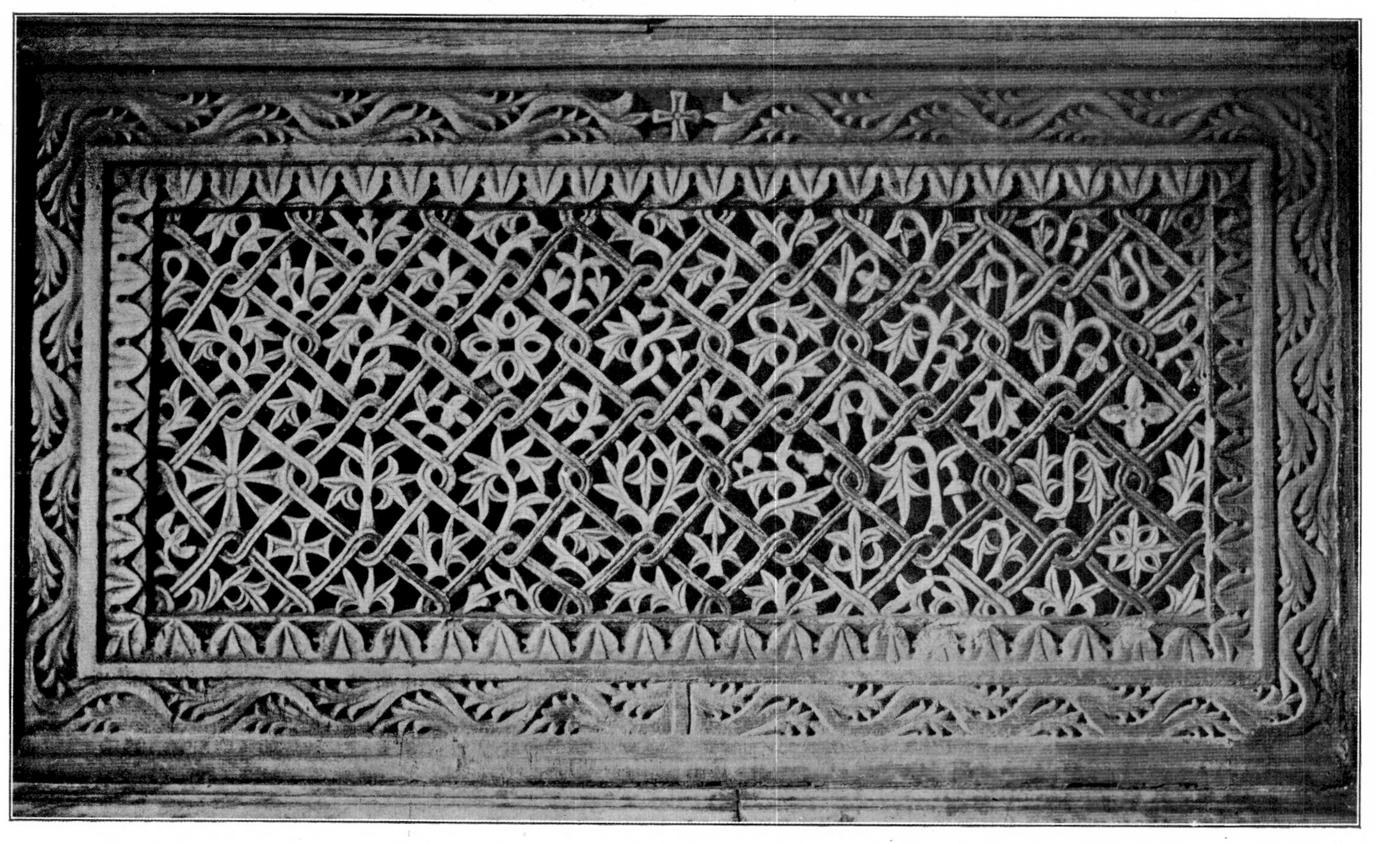

BYZANTINE — MARBLE PANELS FROM RAVENNA. VI CENTURY

BYZANTINE — MARBLE PANELS FROM RAVENNA. VI CENTURY

BYZANTINE — CAPITALS FROM RAVENNA. VI CENTURY

BYZANTINE — CAPITALS FROM PARENZO (ISTRIA). VI CENTURY

BYZANTINE — SARCOPHAGUS FROM RAVENNA. VI CENTURY

BYZANTINE — ALTAR RELIEF FROM RAVENNA. XII CENTURY

BYZANTINE — RELIEF PLATES FROM VENICE. XII CENTURY

1

2

BYZANTINE — 1. RELIEF PLATE FROM RAVENNA. XII CENTURY
2. SARCOPHAGUS FROM RAVENNA. VI CENTURY

BYZANTINE — RELIEF PLATES FROM RAVENNA. XII CENTURY

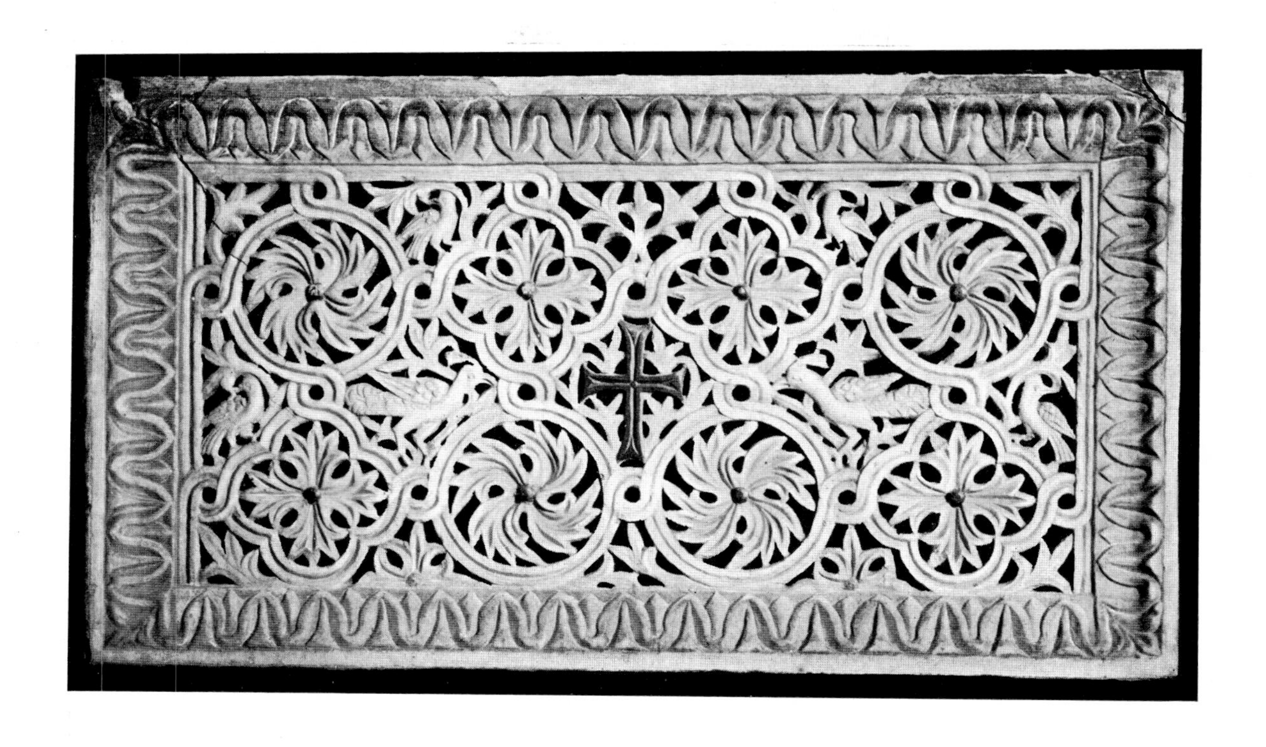

BYZANTINE — RELIEF PLATES FROM RAVENNA. XII CENTURY

BYZANTINE — RELIEF PLATES FROM VENICE. XII AND VII CENTURY

1

2

3

4

5

BYZANTINE CAPITALS — 1. AND 2. FROM GRADO (ISTRIA). VI CENTURY
3. AND 5. FROM S. MARCO IN VENICE. XII CENTURY

BYZANTINE — RELIEF PLATES FROM S. MARCO IN VENICE

1

2

3

BYZANTINE — 1. AND 2. DECORATIVE PLATES. XI—XII CENTURY
3. FOUNTAIN FROM VENICE. XII CENTURY

1

2

3

4

EARLY-CHRISTIAN — 1. AND 2. CAPITALS. VII—IX CENTURY
4. FOUNTAIN. IX CENTURY

1

2

3

1. DECORATIVE PLATE FROM VENICE. VII CENTURY
2. AND 3. CAPITALS. VII—VIII CENTURY

EARLY-CHRISTIAN — RELIEF PLATE FROM CIVIDALE (ISTRIA). 712—749

EARLY-CHRISTIAN — RELIEF PLATE FROM POLA DE LENA (SPAIN). VIII CENTURY

1

2

3

EARLY-CHRISTIAN — 1. AND 3. SARCOPHAGUS. VIII—IX CENTURY. 2. WINDOW-FILLING IN LIME-STONE. X CENTURY

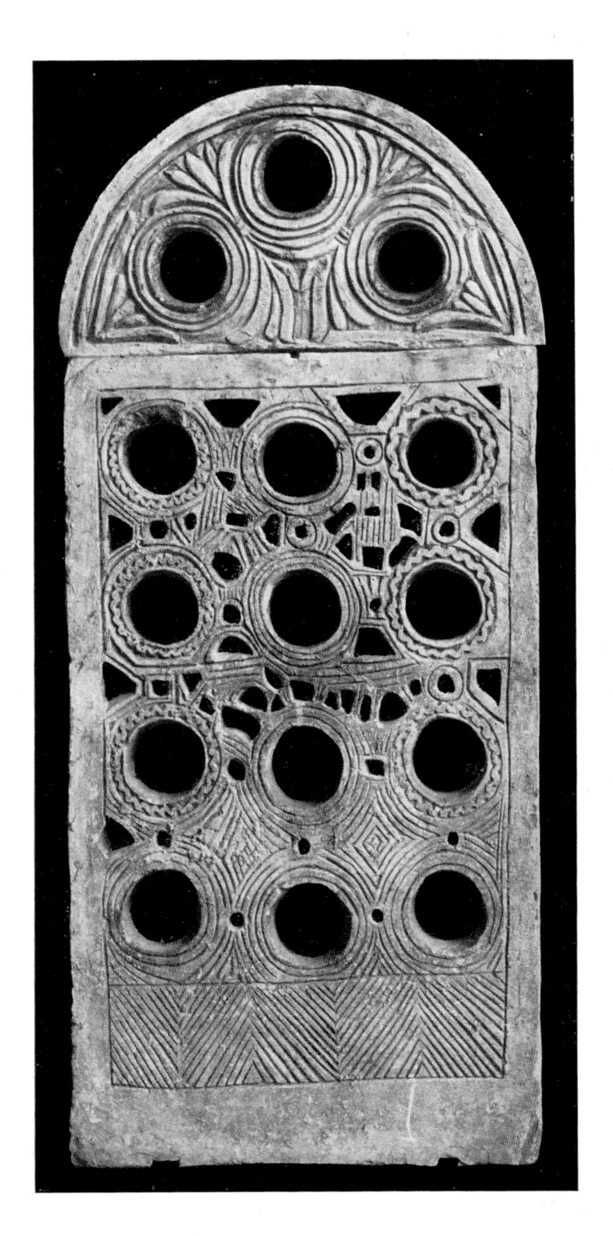

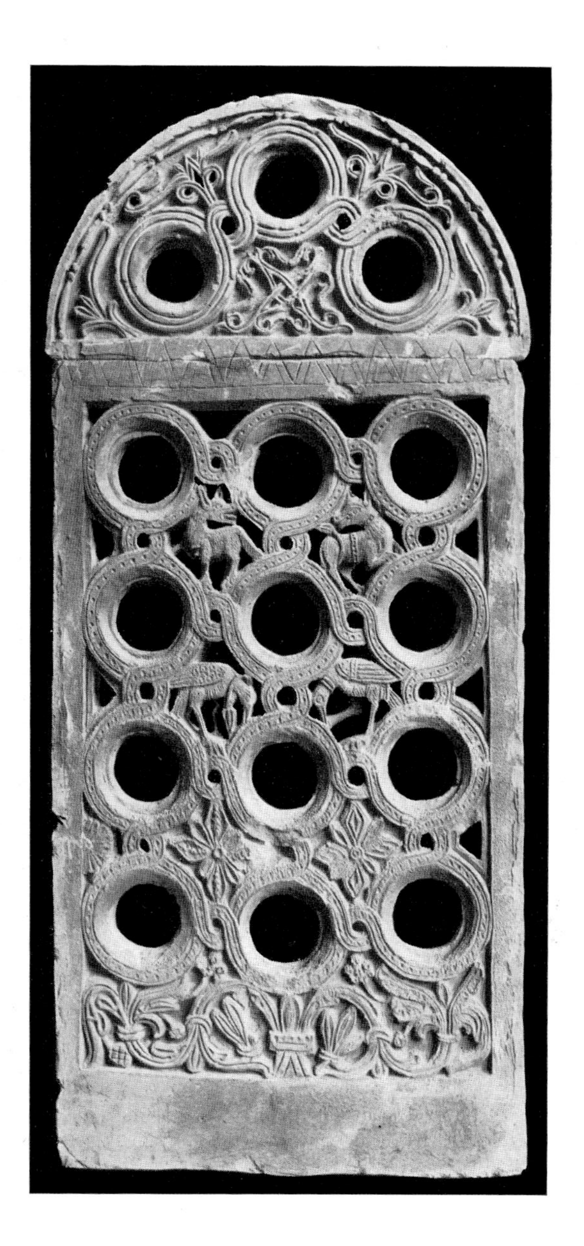

EARLY-CHRISTIAN — WINDOW FILLINGS IN LIME-STONE. X CENTURY

1

2

3

EARLY–CHRISTIAN — 1. AND 2. DECORATIVE PLATES IN LIME–STONE
3. RELIEF: REPRESENTING THE LIGHT TO EGYPT. X CENTURY. DALMATIA

EARLY-CHRISTIAN — PART OF ARCHITECTURE IN LIME-STONE. DALMATIA. X CENTURY

EARLY-CHRISTIAN — DECORATIVE PLATES FROM ISTRIA AND VENICE
VIII AND XI CENTURY

1

2

EARLY-CHRISTIAN — DECORATIVE PLATES. 1. FROM VENICE. XI CENTURY
2. FROM ISTRIA. VIII CENTURY

1

2

1. ROMANESQUE CAPITAL. FRANCE. XI CENTURY. 2. DECORATIVE PLATES FROM ITALY. XII CENTURY

GERMANY, ROMANESQUE — KEYSTONE AND TYMPANUM FROM SOUTH GERMANY. XII CENTURY

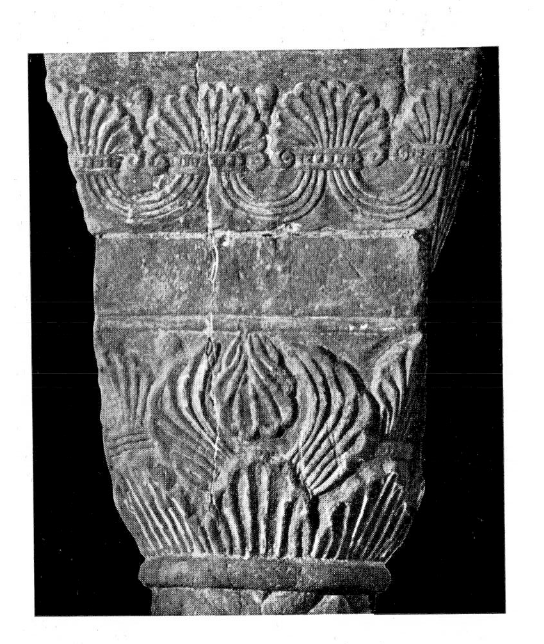

GERMANY, ROMANESQUE — CAPITALS OF ILSENBURG CONVENT. XII CENTURY

GERMANY, ROMANESQUE — CAPITALS FROM THE CASTLE CHURCH AT QUEDLINBURG. XII CENTURY

1

2

FRANCE, ROMANESQUE — 1. CAPITAL FROM ST. DIÉ. XI CENTURY
2. PART OF A CAPITAL FROM MOISSAC. XII CENTURY

GERMANY — PART OF CHOIR PEW FROM THE CHURCH IN LOCCUM (LOWER SAXONY)
ABOUT 1250

GERMANY, ROMANESQUE — CAPITALS FROM THE CASTLE CHURCH AT QUEDLINBURG
XII CENTURY

GERMANY, ROMANESQUE — CAPITALS FROM THE CASTLE CHURCH AT QUEDLINBURG
XII CENTURY

ITALY, ROMANESQUE — PART OF DOORWAY FROM ST. MICHELE, PAVIA
XII CENTURY

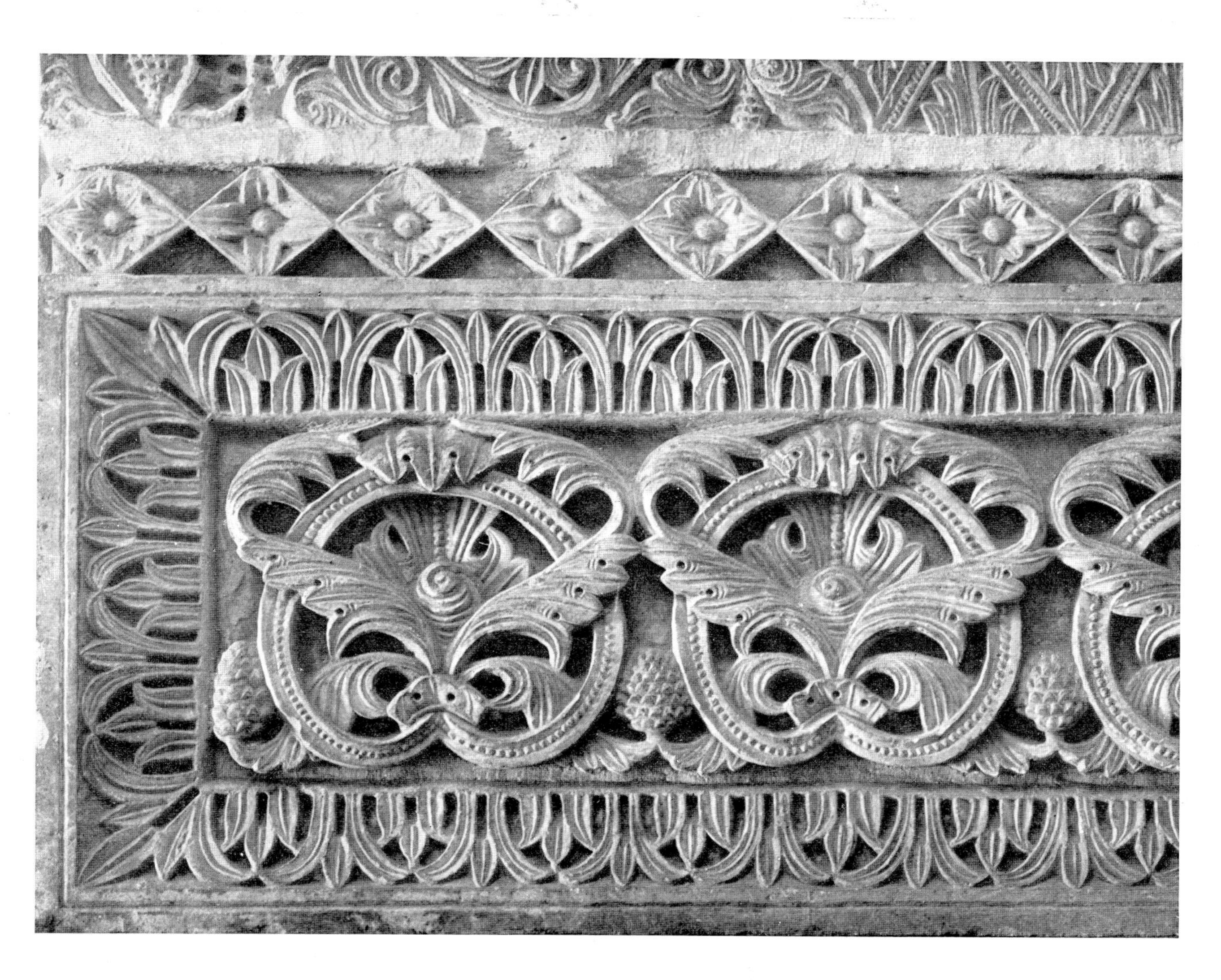

ITALY, ROMANESQUE — PARTS OF ARCHITECTURE FROM VALVE AND LUCCA
XII CENTURY

ITALY, ROMANESQUE — CAPITALS FROM THE BENEDICTINE ABBEY, MONREALE
XII CENTURY

ITALY, ROMANESQUE — CAPITALS FROM THE BENEDICTINE ABBEY, MONREALE
XII CENTURY

FRANCE, ROMANESQUE — PART OF A CHURCH DOORWAY AT AVALLON
XII CENTURY

FRANCE, ROMANESQUE CAPITALS. XII CENTURY

FRANCE, ROMANESQUE — PART OF A CHURCH DOORWAY AT BELLEGARDE
XII CENTURY

FRANCE, ROMANESQUE — PART OF A CHURCH DOORWAY AT ST. MARTIN-LE-BEAU
XII CENTURY

FRANCE, ROMANESQUE — PART OF A CHURCH DOORWAY AT AULNAY
BELOW: PART OF CAPITAL FROM MOISSAC. XII CENTURY

FRANCE, ROMANESQUE — PART OF A CHURCH DOORWAY IN AULNAY
BELOW: PART OF CAPITAL FROM MOISSAC. XII CENTURY

FRANCE, ROMANESQUE — PART OF CHURCH DOORWAY IN AULNAY. XII CENTURY

FRANCE, ROMANESQUE — PART OF FAÇADE OF THE CHURCH IN LE DOUHET. XII CENTURY

FRANCE, ROMANESQUE — DOORWAY FIGURE FROM ST. PIERRE IN MOISSAC. XII CENTURY

FRANCE, ROMANESQUE — DOORWAY FIGURE FROM ST. PIERRE IN MOISSAC. XII CENTURY

FRANCE, ROMANESQUE — PARTS OF ARCHITECTURE FROM ROUEN
XII CENTURY

FRANCE, ROMANESQUE — PART OF CHURCH DOORWAY IN COGNAC. XII CENTURY

FRANCE, ROMANESQUE — PART OF FAÇADE OF ST. PIERRE IN ANGOULEME. XII CENTURY

FRANCE, ROMANESQUE — PART OF DOORWAY OF THE CATHEDRALE IN BOURGES. XII CENTURY

FRANCE, ROMANESQUE — PART OF DOORWAY OF THE CATHEDRAL IN BOURGES
XII CENTURY

FRANCE, ROMANESQUE — PART OF DOORWAY FROM ST. DENIS
XII CENTURY

FRANCE, ROMANESQUE — TYMPANUM RELIEF FROM ANGOULEME (MUSEUM). XII CENTURY

FRANCE, ROMANESQUE — PART OF DOORWAY FROM ST. DENIS. XII CENTURY

FRANCE, ROMANESQUE — PART OF DOORWAY OF ST. PIERRE IN MELLE. XII CENTURY

FRANCE, ROMANESQUE — DOORWAY FIGURES FROM ST. DENIS. XII CENTURY

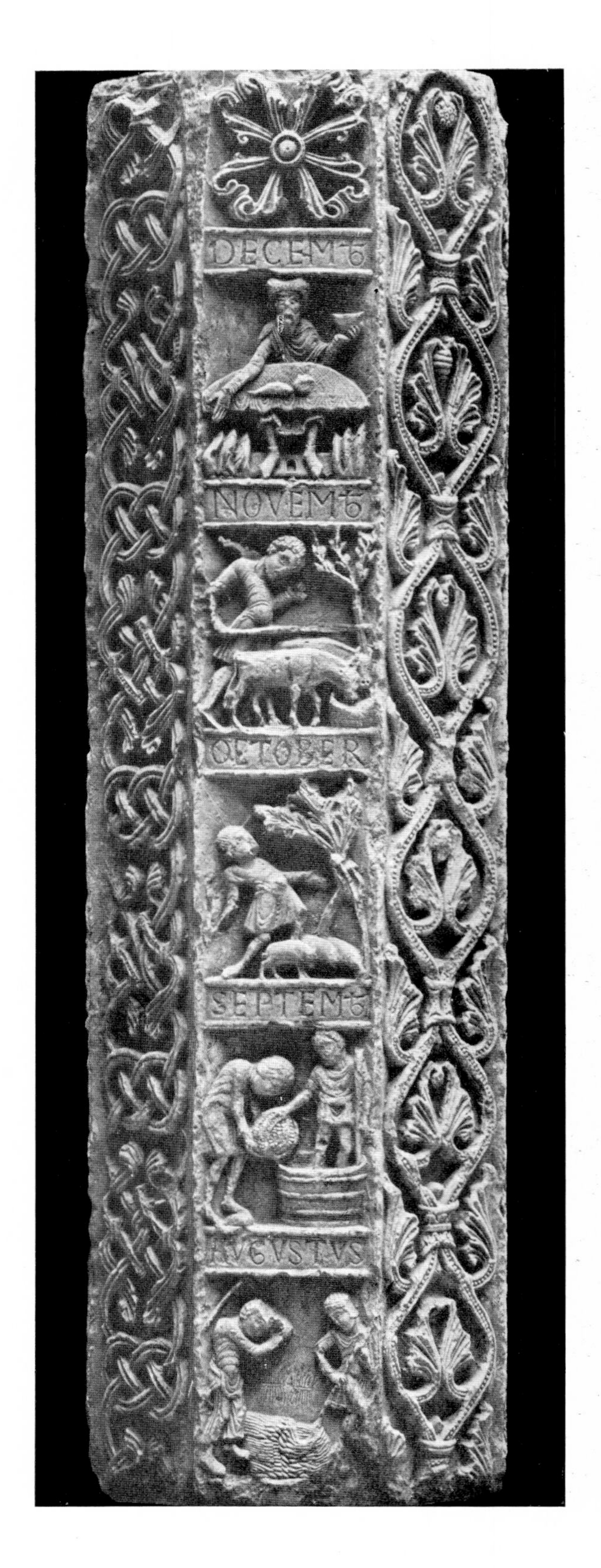

FRANCE, ROMANESQUE — PARTS OF DOORWAY FROM THE CHURCH IN SOUVIGNY. XII CENTURY

FRANCE, ROMANESQUE — PILASTER FROM THE CHURCH FAÇADE AT ST. GILLES
XII CENTURY

1

2

FRANCE, ROMANESQUE — 1. RELIEF ON THE CHURCH DOORWAY AT ST. GILLES
2. CAPITAL FROM ST. SERNIN AT TOULOUSE. XII CENTURY

FRANCE, ROMANESQUE — CAPITALS FROM TOULOUSE (MUSEUM) AND MOISSAC
XII CENTURY

ITALY — DOORWAY DECORATION FROM ST. MARCO, VENICE. XIII CENTURY

ITALY — DOORWAY DECORATION FROM ST. MARCO, VENICE. XIII CENTURY

GERMANY, LATE–ROMANESQUE — CAPITALS FROM GELNHAUSEN. XIII CENTURY

GERMANY, LATE-ROMANESQUE — CAPITALS FROM GELNHAUSEN. XIII CENTURY

GERMANY, LATE-ROMANESQUE — CAPITALS FROM THE DOM AT NAUMBURG
XIII CENTURY

GERMANY, LATE–ROMANESQUE — CAPITALS FROM THE DOM AT NAUMBURG

ENGLAND, EARLY-GOTHIC — PARTS OF ARCHITECTURE FROM THE CATHEDRAL AT WELLS. END OF XIII CENTURY

GERMANY, EARLY-GOTHIC — DOORWAY TYNPANUM ON THE DOM AT MAGDEBURG
XIII CENTURY

FRANCE, GOTHIC — SCULPTURAL DETAILS ON THE TOWER PARAPET OF NOTRE DAME, PARIS. XIII CENTURY

FRANCE, GOTHIC — DOORWAY AND FAÇADE DECORATION FROM THE CATHEDRAL AT SCEZ. XIII CENTURY

FRANCE, GOTHIC — DECORATIVE DETAILS FROM THE CATHEDRALS AT PARIS, REIMS AND NEVERS. XIII CENTURY

FRANCE, GOTHIC — DECORATIVE DETAILS FROM THE CATHEDRALS AT PARIS AND DIJON. XIII CENTURY

FRANCE, GOTHIC — ARCHITEKTURAL DETAILS, REIMS CATHEDRAL
AND NOTRE DAME, PARIS. XIII CENTURY

FRANCE, GOTHIC — CAPITAL AND MOULDING, RHEIMS CATHEDRAL. XIII CENTURY

FRANCE, GOTHIC — FIGURE OF A PROPHET FROM REIMS CATHEDRAL
XIII CENTURY

FRANCE, GOTHIC — FIGURE OF A PROPHET FROM REIMS CATHEDRAL
XIII CENTURY

FRANCE, GOTHIC — CAPITAL AND FRIEZE, RHEIMS CATHEDRAL. XIII CENTURY

FRANCE, GOTHIC — SURFACE ORNAMENT ON MAIN DOORWAY, RHEIMS CATHEDRAL. XIII CENTURY

FRANCE, GOTHIC — DOORWAY DECORATION FROM THE CATHEDRAL AT LE MANS
XIII CENTURY

FRANCE, GOTHIC — DETAIL OF PORTAL, AMIENS CATHEDRAL. XIII CENTURY

GERMANY, GOTHIC — CORBET, HAINA CHURCH (HESSE). END OF XIII CENTURY

GERMANY, GOTHIC — CAPITALS, NAUMBURG CATHEDRAL. XIII CENTURY

GERMANY, GOTHIC — CAPITALS, NAUMBURG CATHEDRAL. XIII CENTURY

GERMANY, GOTHIC — CAPITALS, NAUMBURG CATHEDRAL. XIII CENTURY

BÂLE, GOTHIC — ST. GEORGE, ON THE FAÇADE OF THE MINSTER. XIV CENTURY

BÂLE, GOTHIC — ST. MARTIN, ON THE FAÇADE OF THE MINSTER. XIV CENTURY

GERMANY, GOTHIC — RELIEFS, TOWER FRIEZE, STRASSBURG CATHEDRAL END OF XIV CENTURY

GERMANY, GOTHIC — GARGOYLE, KILIAN CHURCH, HEILBRONN. XIV CENTURY

FRANCE, GOTHIC — ARCHITECTURAL DETAILS, NOTRE DAME AND CARM CHURCH
XIV CENTURY

FRANCE, GOTHIC — CONSOLES. AMIENS CATHEDRAL. XIII CENTURY

GERMANY, GOTHIC — RELIEFS, FORMER "KAUFHAUS", MAYENCE. 1320

ENGLAND, GOTHIC — BOSSES. XV CENTURY

GERMANY, GOTHIC — DETAIL FROM STALL, S. GERMANY. XV CENTURY

FRANCE, GOTHIC — MISERERES FROM A STALL IN AMIENS. XIV CENTURY

FRANCE, GOTHIC — PILASTER PANELS, WOOD. XIV CENTURY

GERMANY, LATE GOTHIC — PIERCED PANEL, LOWER GERMANY. XV CENTURY

FRANCE, GOTHIC — CAPITAL AND CONSOLE. XV CENTURY. TROYES MUSEUM

FRANCE, GOTHIC — DETAIL OF PORTAL ORNAMENT, HÔTEL DE CLUNY, PARIS
XV CENTURY

FRANCE, GOTHIC — FRIEZE AND CONSOLE, ST. MARTIN DES CHAMPS, PARIS
XIII CENTURY

FRANCE, LATE GOTHIC — CONSOLES FROM PORTAL OF ST. NICOLAS DES CHAMPS, PARIS. XV CENTURY

ITALY — RELIEFS BY ANDREA PISANO ON THE CAMPANILE, FLORENCE
XIV CENTURY

ITALY — RELIEFS BY ANDREA PISANO ON THE CAMPANILE, FLORENCE
XIV CENTURY

ITALY — RELIEFS BY ANDREA PISANO ON THE CAMPANILE, FLORENCE
XIV CENTURY

ITALY — RELIEFS BY ANDREA PISANO ON THE CAMPANILE, FLORENCE
XIV CENTURY

ITALY — BRONZE RELIEF BY GHIBERTI. BAPTISTERY, FLORENCE
XV CENTURY

ITALY, RENAISSANCE — BRONZE RELIEF BY GHIBERTI. BAPTISTERY, FLORENCE
XV CENTURY

MARBLE ROSETTES, ARCHBISHOP'S PALACE, PISA. XV CENTURY

MARBLE ROSETTES, ARCHBISHOP'S PALACE, PISA. XV CENTURY

ITALY, RENAISSANCE — TORCH-HOLDER, BRONZE. FLORENCE 1503

ITALY, RENAISSANCE — PORTAL DECORATION, BAPTISTERY, PARMA. XV CENTURY

ITALY, RENAISSANCE — CAPITAL, PALAZZO VINEZIA, ROME. XV CENTURY

1

2

3

ITALY, RENAISSANCE — 1. COAT OF ARMS OF MERCHANTS AT PISA
2. AND 3. FAMILY ESCUTCHEONS, FLORENCE. XV CENTURY

ITALY, RENAISSANCE — CAPITALS, FLORENCE. XV CENTURY

CAPITALS FROM THE RECTOR'S PALACE, RAGUSA (DALMATIA). XV CENTURY

ITALY, RENAISSANCE — CAPITALS FROM FLORENCE AND PAVIA. XV CENTURY

ITALY, RENAISSANCE — CAPITALS, FLORENCE. XV CENTURY

ITALY, RENAISSANCE — STAIRCASE IN THE PALAZZO GONDI, FLORENCE. XV CENTURY

ITALY, RENAISSANCE — CEILING IN THE ACCADEMIA, VENICE. XV CENTURY

ITALY, RENAISSANCE — PIERCED BALUSTRADE PANELS, FLORENCE AND VENICE
XV CENTURY

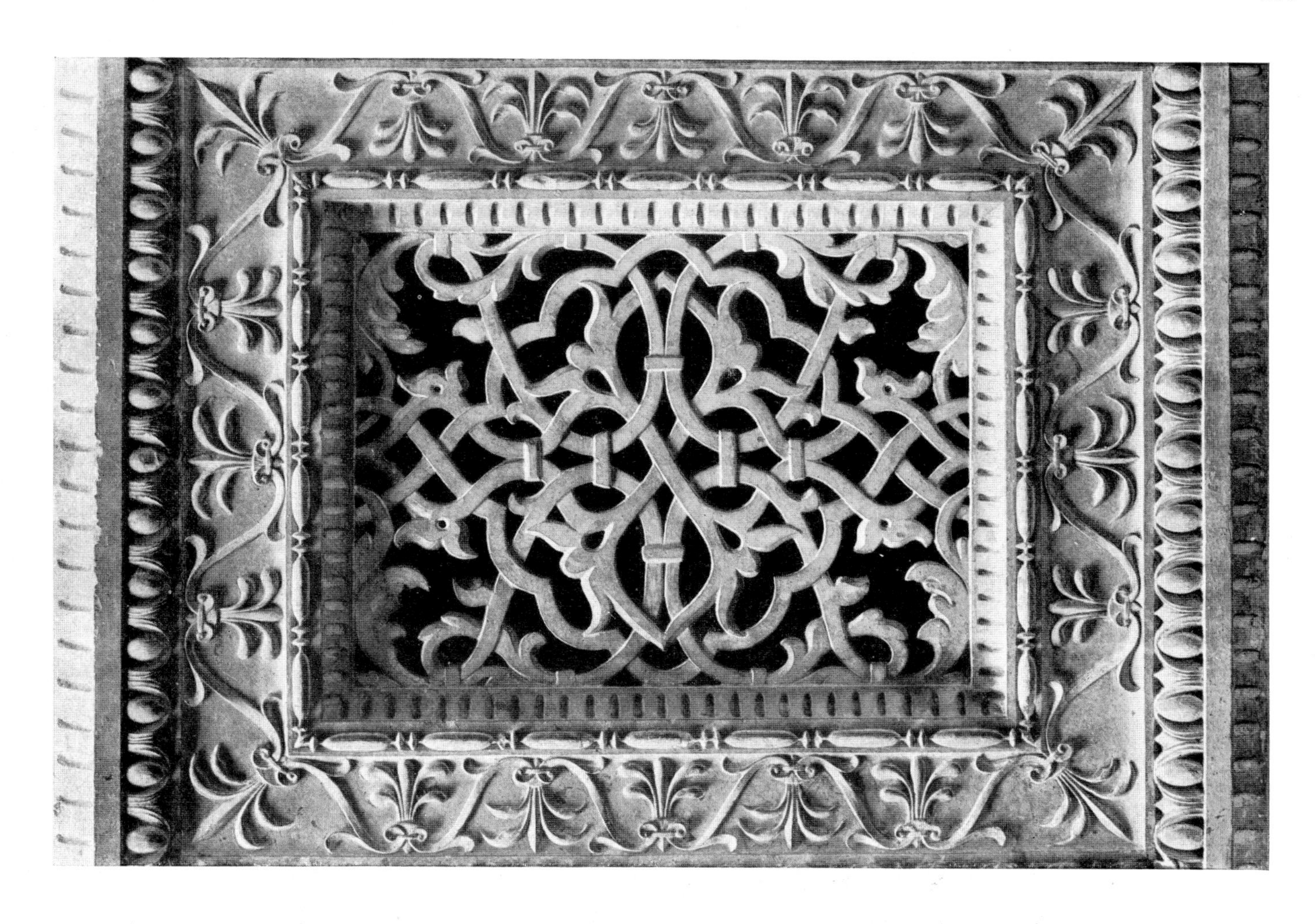

ITALY, RENAISSANCE — PIERCED BALUSTRADE PANELS, URBINE AND VENICE. XV CENTURY

ITALY, RENAISSANCE — PILASTER CAPITALS, FLORENCE. XV CENTURY

ITALY, XIV CENTURY. — CONSOLES FROM CASTEL MONDOLFO (VICTORIA AND ALBERTMUSEUM, LONDON)

ITALY, RENAISSANCE — FAÇADE ORNAMENT, PALAZZO DI PODESTA, BOLOGNA
XV CENTURY

ITALY, RENAISSANCE — DOORWAY, PALAZZO MARTINENGO, BRESCIA. XV CENTURY

ITALY, RENAISSANCE — FOUNTAIN, PALAZZO BEVILAQUA, BOLOGNA. XV CENTURY

ITALY, FOUNTAIN IN PRATO. XVI CENTURY

ITALY — FOUNTAIN HERMES IN THE PALAZZO BORGHESE GARDEN. XVI CENTURY

ITALY — CARYATIDES, FLORENCE. XVI CENTURY

ITALY — FAÇADE ORNAMENT, S. BERNARDINO, PERUGIA. XV CENTURY

ITALY — CANDELABRUM ORNAMENT, DUCAL PALACE, URBINO. XVI CENTURY

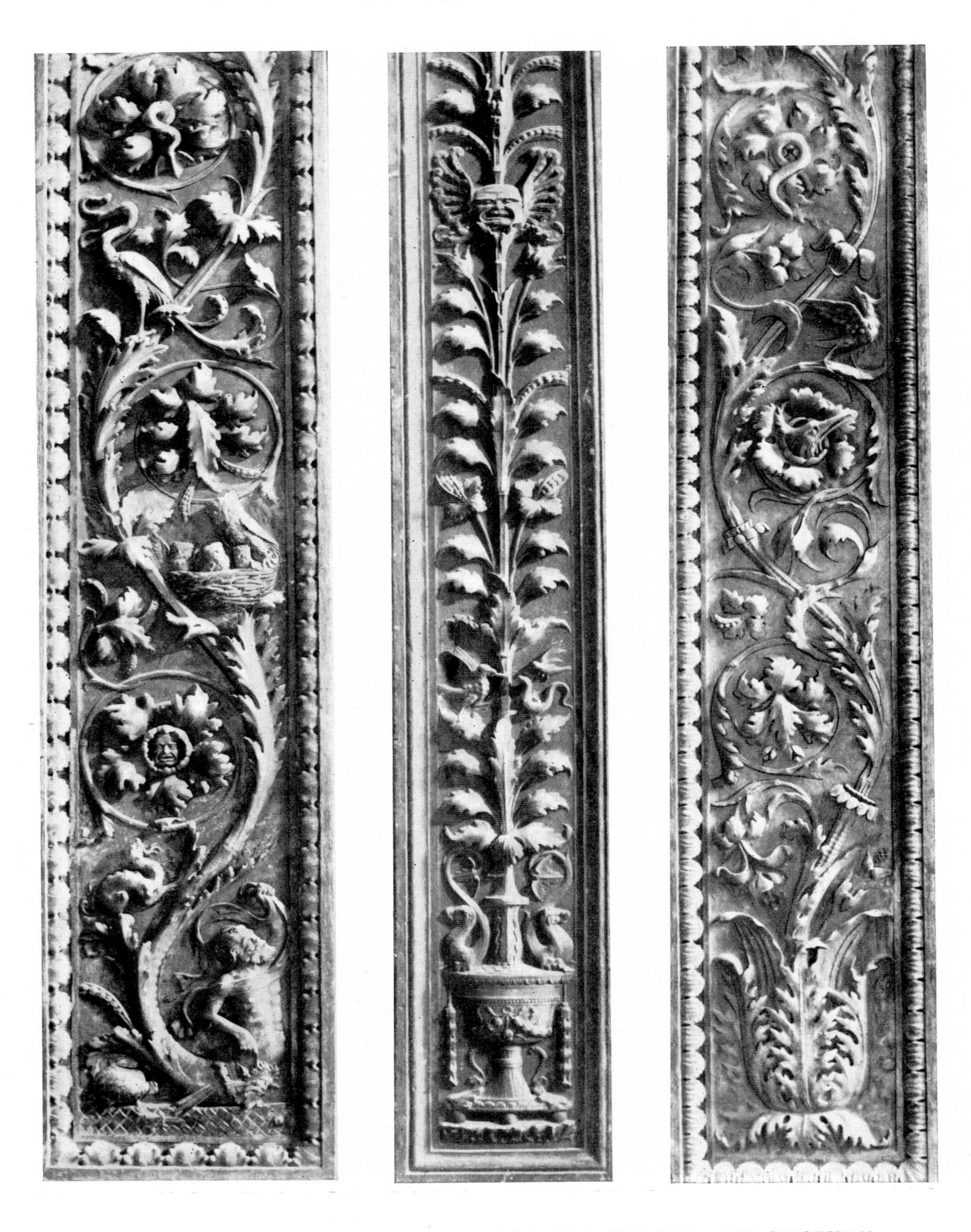

ITALY — PILASTER PANELS, S. ANASTASIA, VERONA. XV CENTURY

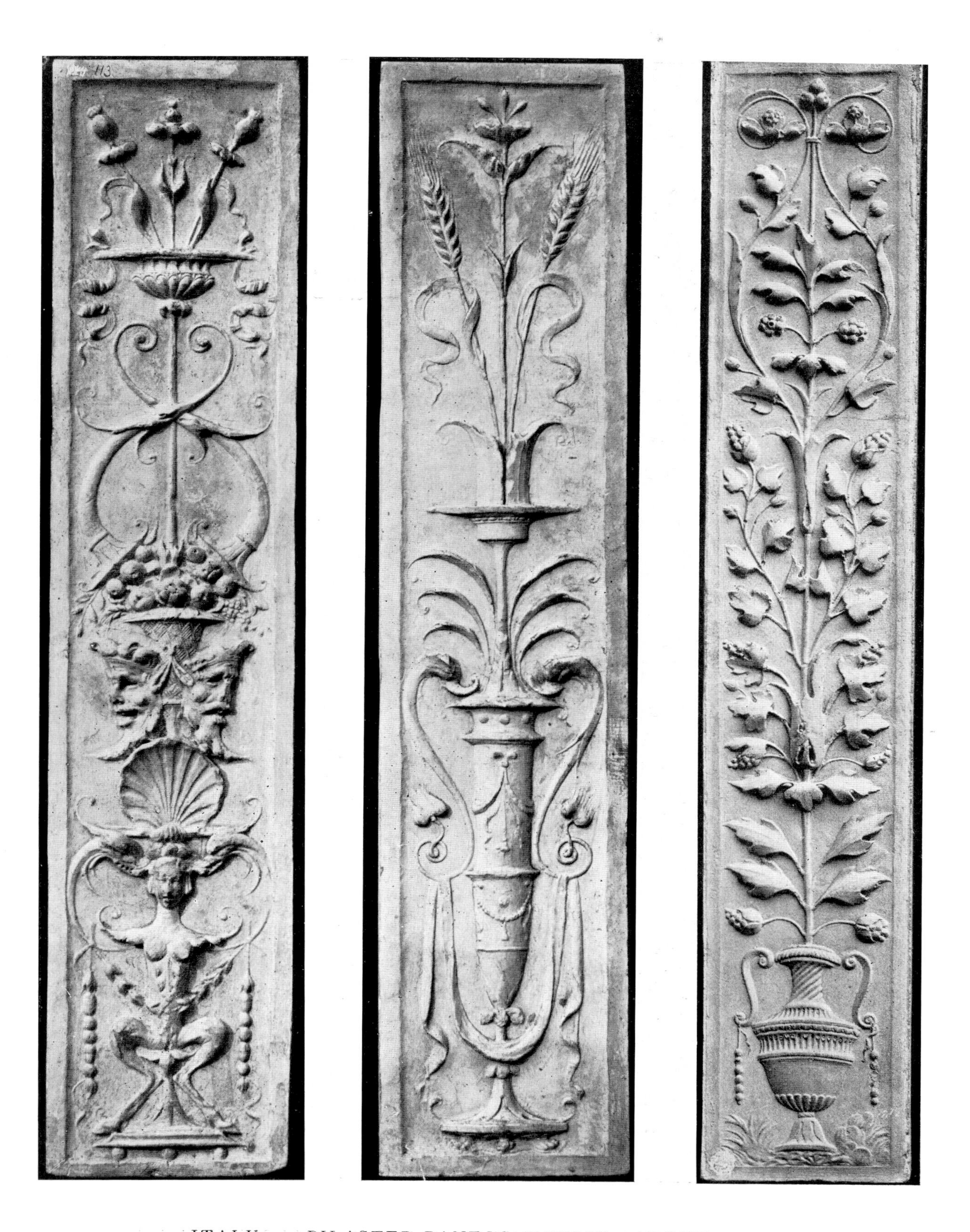

ITALY, — PILASTER PANELS, VENICE. ABOUT 1500

ITALY — RELIEF FROM THE STAIRWAY IN THE PALAZZO DUCALE, VENICE
XVI CENTURY

ITALY — PILASTER PANELS, VERONA, S. ANASTASIA — XV CENTURY

ITALY — FRIEZES FROM PERUGIA AND VENICE. XV CENTURY

ITALY — BAS-RELIEF FROM FERRARA. XV CENTURY

ITALY — CONSOLE FROM SABBIONETA (MANTUA). XVI CENTURY

ITALY — PANEL CONSOLES. XVI CENTURY

ITALY — DETAILS OF A STALL, S. PIETRO, PERUGIA. XVI CENTURY

ITALY — DETAILS OF A STALL, S. PIETRO, PERUGIA. XVI CENTURY

GERMANY — DETAILS OF A STALL, MAYENCE CATHEDRAL. ABOUT 1570

GERMANY — DETAILS OF A STALL, MAYENCE CATHEDRAL. ABOUT 1570

GERMANY — COAT OF ARMS (SOLNHOFEN STONE) BY HANS DAUHER
XVI CENTURY

GERMANY — COAT OF ARMS (SOLNHOFEN STONE) BY HANS DAUHER
XVI CENTURY

FRANCE — CARYATIDES FROM DE PIERRE HOUSE, TOULOUSE. XVI CENTURY

FRANCE — CARYATIDES FROM LABORDES HOUSE TOULOUSE. XVI CENTURY

FRANCE — RELIEFS, NOTRE DAME DE CHARTRES. XVI CENTURY

FRANCE — RELIEFS, NOTRE DAME DE CHARTRES. XVI CENTURY

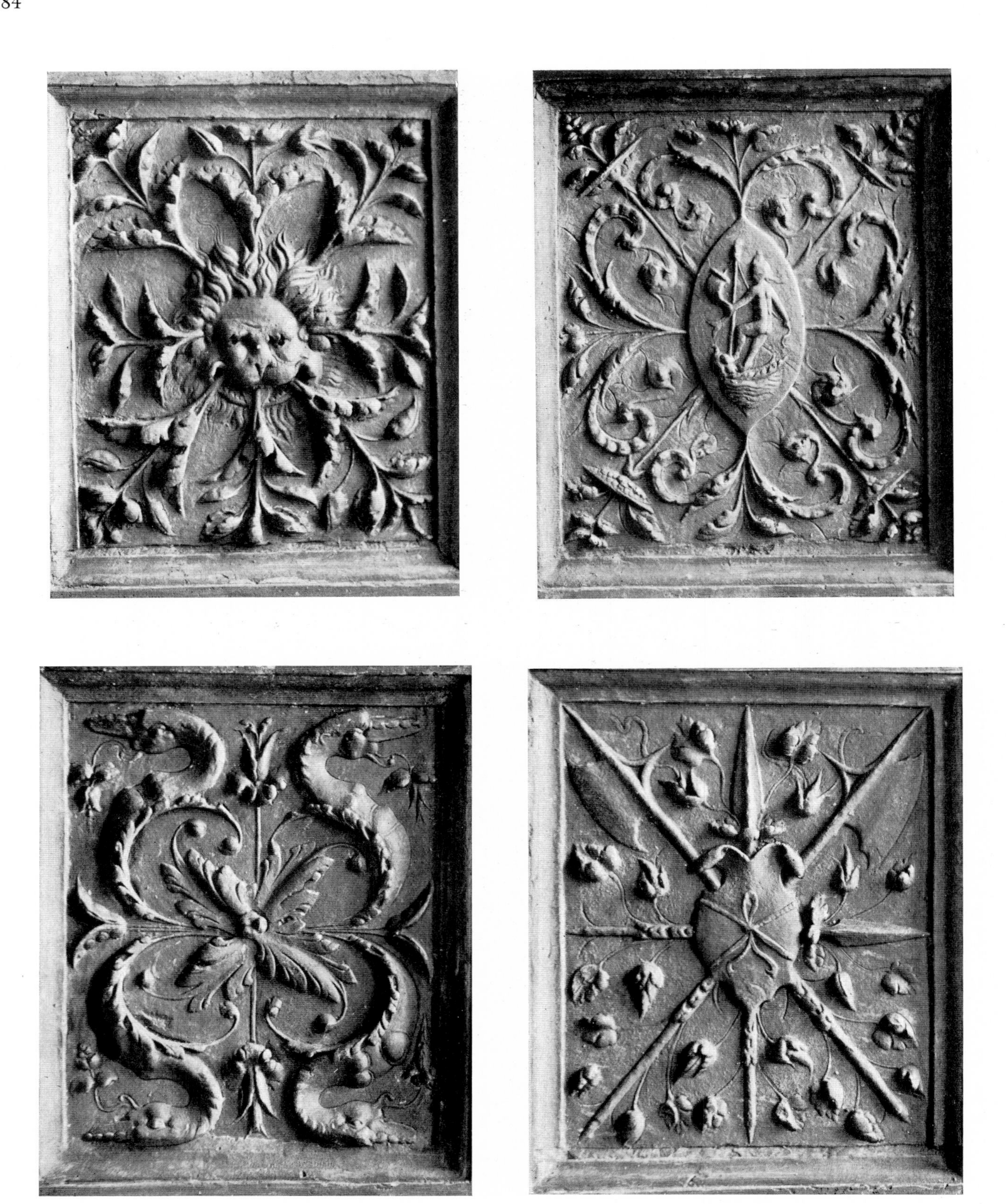

FRANCE — STONE LACUNARS FROM A CEILING IN ORLEANS. XVI CENTURY

FRANCE — FAÇADE ORNAMENT, LAON CATHEDRAL. XVI CENTURY

FRANCE — DETAIL OF WOOD CARVING ON A DOOR, CHATEAU D'ANET
XVI CENTURY

FRANCE — RELIEF ON WAINSCOTING. XVI CENTURY

FRANCE, BURGUNDY — CARYATIDES (WOOD), HOENTSCHEL COLLECTION, NEW YORK
XVI CENTURY

ISLAMIC ORNAMENT

1

2

1. FRAGMENT OF A FRIEZE FROM PERSIA. VI CENTURY
2. RELIEF FROM S. ARABIA. V CENTURY

EARLY ISLAMIC — STUCCO RELIEFS WITH RAM AND BIRD
PERSIA, VII–VIII CENTURY

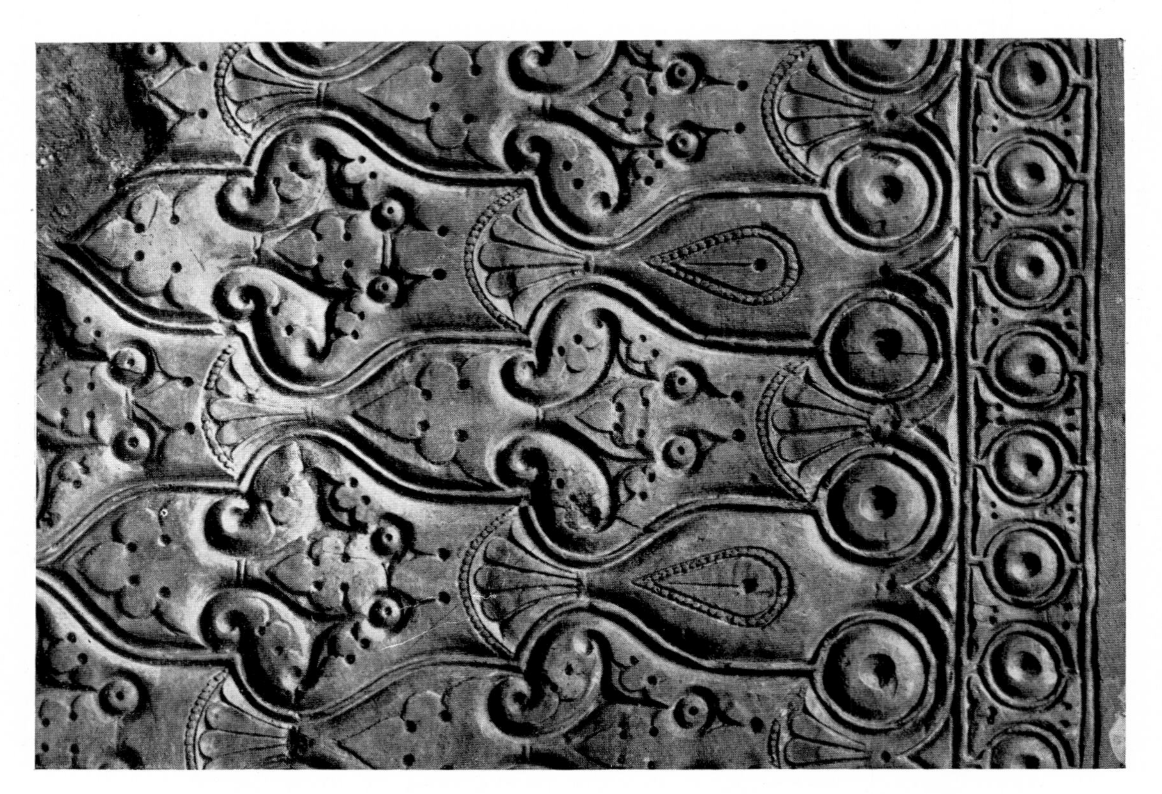

STUCCO ORNAMENT FROM SAMARA. IX CENTURY

STUCCO ORNAMENT FROM SAMARA. IX CENTURY

WOOD CARVINGS FROM EGYPT (SAMARA STYLE). IX CENTURY

WOOD AND STUCCO ORNAMENT FROM EGYPT. XI–XII CENTURY

WOOD CARVINGS FROM EGYPT. VIII CENTURY

WOOD CARVINGS FROM EGYPT. XI–XII CENTURY

IVORIES FROM BAGDAD. XII CENTURY

IVORIES FROM BAGDAD. XII CENTURY

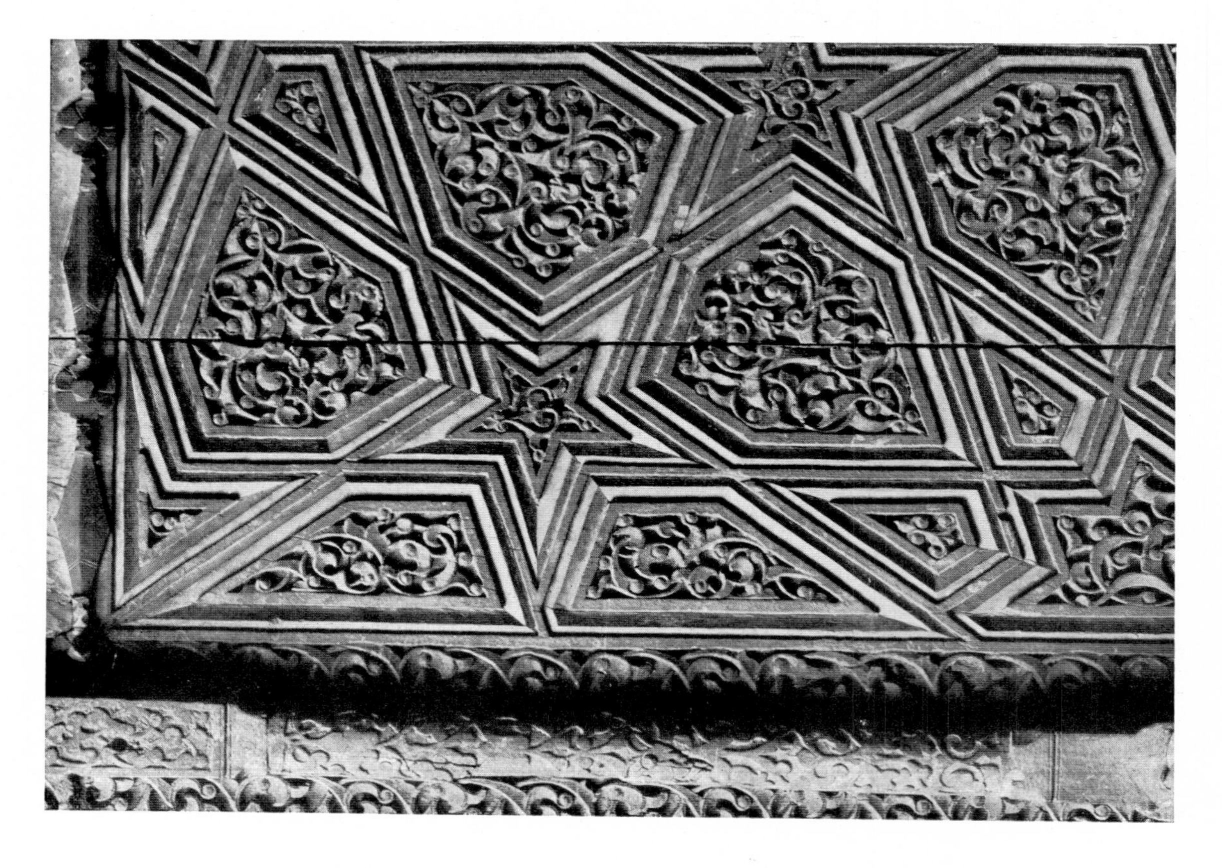

WOOD CARVINGS FROM KONYA. XIII CENTURY

WOOD CARVINGS FROM EGYPT. XIII CENTURY

PERSIA — PRAYER NICHE, MARAND MOSQUE. XIII CENTURY

PART OF THE ENTRANCE NICHE OF A MOSQUE IN SAMARKAND
XIII CENTURY

ARCHITECTURAL DETAILS FROM EGYPT AND INDIA. XIII CENTURY

ISLAMIC ORNAMENT: SYRIA AND EGYPT — ARCHITECTURAL DETAILS
XIV CENTURY

ISLAMIC — WINDOW, MAUSOLEUM IN AHMEDABAD. XV CENTURY

ISLAMIC ORNAMENT: SYRIA — MOSQUE NICHE. XV CENTURY

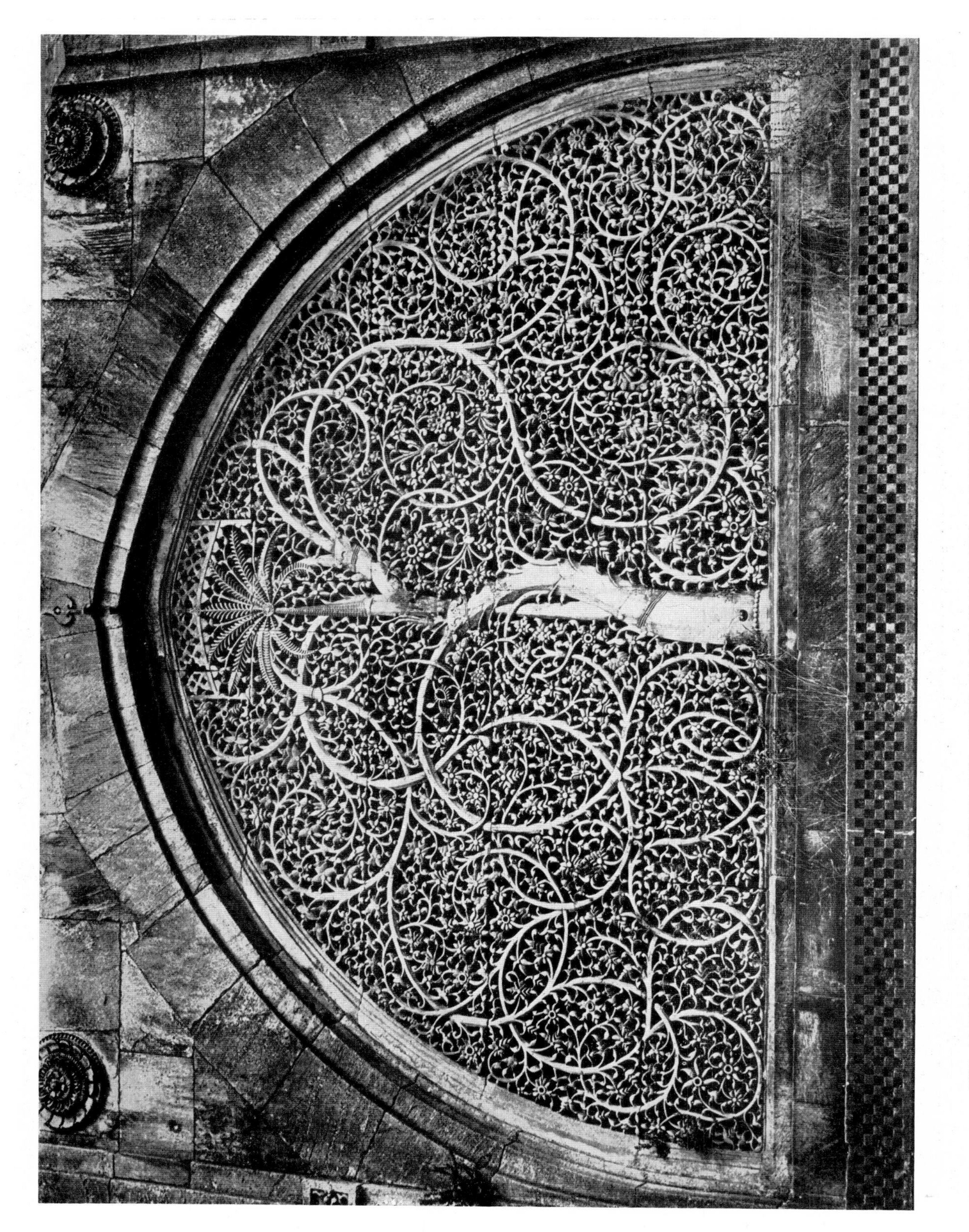

ISLAMIC — MARBLE WINDOW, SIDI SAID MOSQUE, ADSHMEDABAD. XV CENTURY

ISLAMIC, MOORISH — STUCCO DECORATION, MAUSOLEUM, MERAKESH. XVI CENTURY

ISLAMIC, MOORISH — STUCCO DECORATION, MERAKESH, MAUSOLEUM. XVI CENTURY

ISLAMIC, MOORISH — STUCCO DECORATION, FEZ. XVI CENTURY

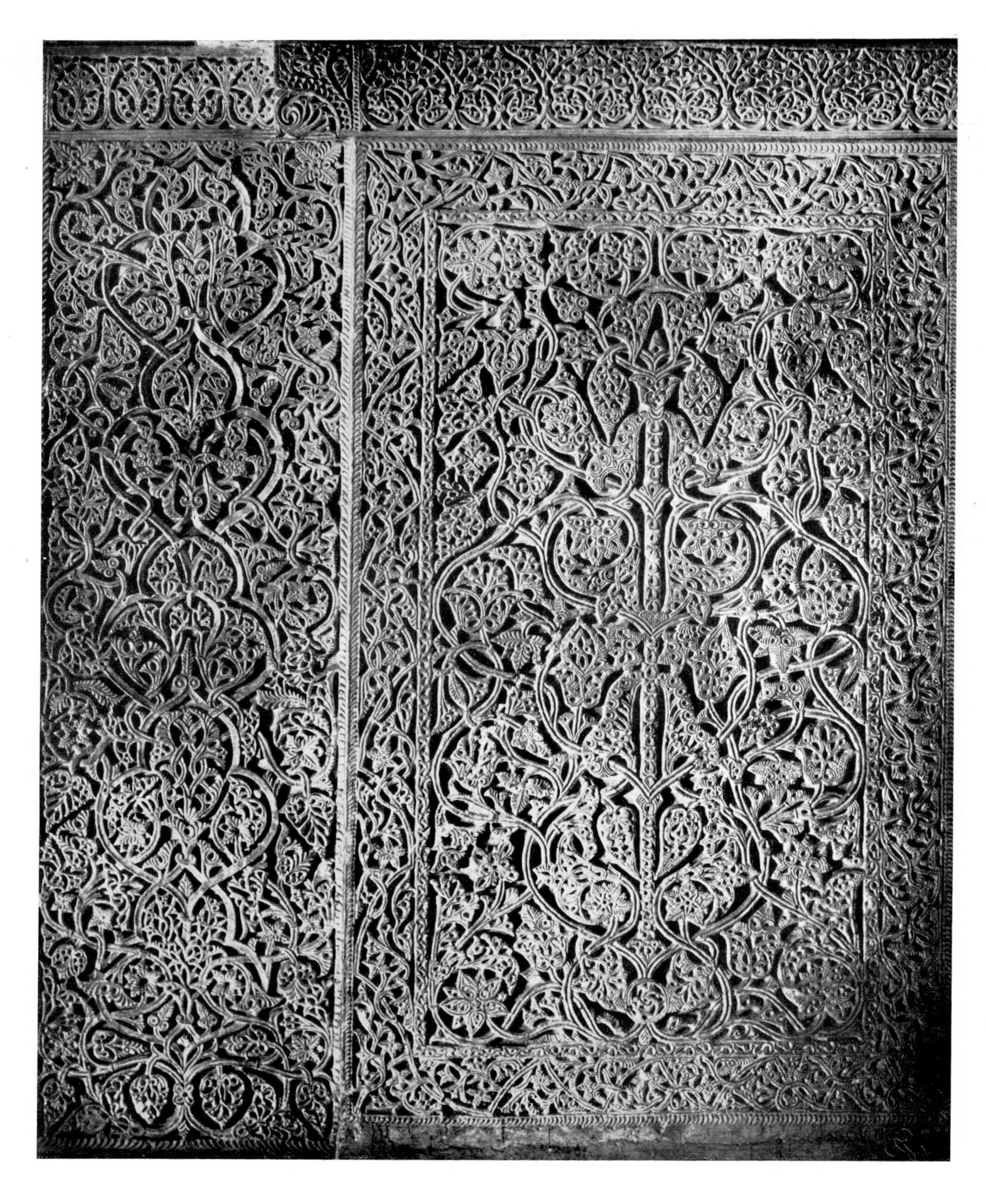

ISLAMIC, OMMIAD STYLE — MARBLE DECORATION. CORDOBA: MEZQUITA
ABOUT 970

ISLAMIC, MOORISH — STUCCO DECORATION, ALHAMBRA, GRANADA. XIV CENTURY

ISLAMIC, MOORISH — DETAIL FROM THE LIONS' COURT, ALHAMBRA, GRANADA
XIV CENTURY

ISLAMIC, MOORISH — DETAIL FROM THE LIONS' COURT, ALHAMBRA, GRANADA
XIV CENTURY

ISLAMIC, MOORISH — DETAIL OF CAPITAL IN THE LIONS' COURT, ALHAMBRA GRANADA. XIV CENTURY

ISLAMIC, MOORISH — CAPITAL IN THE LIONS' COURT, ALHAMBRA, GRANADA
XIV CENTURY

ISLAMIC, MUDEJAR STYLE — SPRINGING OF AN ARCH, SEVILLA, ALCAZAR
XVI CENTURY

ISLAMIC, MOORISH — CAPITALS. MAUSOLEUM, MERAKESH. XVI CENTURY

ISLAMIC, MUDEJAR STYLE.— CAPITALS IN SANTA MARIA BLANCA (FORMERLY THE SYNAGOGUE), TOLEDO. XIII CENTURY

160 Pl.